1954

THE REFERENCE SHEL

Volume X

No.
5. Federal World Government. J. E. Johnsen. $1.50.
6. Federal Information Controls in Peacetime. R. E. Summers. $1.50.

No.
7. Should the Communist Party Be Outlawed? J. E. Johnsen. $1.50.

Volume XIX

No.
3. Free Medical Care. C. A. Peters. $1.25.

No.
5. United Nations or World Government. J. E. Johnsen. 75c.

Volume XVIII

No.
3. Representative American Speeches: 1945-1946. A. C. Baird. $1.25.
5. Anatomy of Racial Intolerance. G. B. de Huszar. $1.25.

No.
6. Palestine: Jewish Homeland? J. E. Johnsen. $1.25.

Volume XVII

No.
4. Representative American Speeches: 1943-1944. A. C. Baird. $1.25.

No.
5. Lowering the Voting Age. J. E. Johnsen. $1.25.

Volume XVI

No.
1. Representative American Speeches: 1941-1942. A. C. Baird. $1.25.
2. Plans for a Postwar World. J. E. Johnsen. 50c.

No.
6. Representative American Speeches: 1942-1943. A. C. Baird. $1.25.
7. Reconstituting the League of Nations. J. E. Johnsen. 50c.

Volume XV

No.
1. Representative American Speeches: 1940-1941. A. C. Baird. $1.25.
2. Universal Military Service. R. E. Summers and H. B. Summers. $1.25.
3. Federal Regulation of Labor Unions. J. V. Garland. $1.25.

No.
7. The Closed Shop. J. E. Johnsen. $1.25.
9. Permanent Price Control Policy. J. E. Johnsen. $1.25.
10. A Federal Sales Tax. E. R. Nichols. $1.25.

THE REFERENCE SHELF

Vol. 25   No. 4

PRESIDENTIAL ELECTION REFORMS

Edited by
WALTER M. DANIELS
Foreign News Staff, The New York Times

THE H. W. WILSON COMPANY
NEW YORK   1953

PREFACE

This compilation deals with the National University Extension Association "problem area" for the academic year 1953-1954, namely, How should we select the President of the United States? Its objects are (1) to give a picture of the process of choosing a President in all its stages, and (2) to present the proposals now before Congress for reforms in that process.

It is oversimplification to think of electoral reform merely as amendment of our Constitution and statutes. The purpose of reform proposals is to give the people a more direct voice in choosing their President. But the voter who complains in November that his choice is limited to two party-picked candidates has neglected his opportunities in April and July to take a more active part in the picking. Too many Americans are content to leave the nominating process to the politicians.

Some delegates to the Constitutional Convention of 1787 wanted to let the people directly choose their President. Others, fearing the evil effects of party politics, as observed in Europe, upon public sentiment, favored letting Congress make the selection. The electoral college was a compromise. It was anticipated, by the opponents of popular election, that this elite group of leaders from each of the states would propose for the presidency several of the best qualified citizens, but, being unable to agree on any one of them, would pass along this task to the House of Representatives.

The compromise system did, indeed, work just about like that in the first two elections. Then political parties came into the picture, as feared by the foes of popular election. Since then parties have dominated the electoral process, while a continuous struggle has gone on to adapt the system to circumstances it was not designed to cope with.

The first section of this volume deals with the structure and functioning of parties and how they became the keystone of our political structure. The second section describes how presidential candidates are chosen and how party conventions work. It weighs the primary as a means of selecting delegates to party conventions and as a reflection of popular support for presidential aspirants. The third section deals with the campaign, its almost incredible costliness, the tremendous burden it places on candidates, and its effectiveness in influencing votes. The fourth section describes actual election procedure, centering around the electoral college, and discusses proposals for reform of this system. Constitutional and statutory provisions governing election of the President are given textually in an appendix, followed by a bibliography of sources from which material in this book was drawn and of supplementary reading.

The compiler expresses his sincere thanks to publishers and authors who have given permission for reproduction of the articles here presented.

WALTER M. DANIELS

June 20, 1953

CONTENTS

PREFACE 3

THE PARTY SYSTEM

Editor's Introduction 9
McHenry, Dean E. How Political Parties Function .. Annals
    of the American Academy of Political and Social Science   9
Flynn, Edward J. Why Machines and Bosses? ....
.... Atlantic Monthly   14
How Candidates Are Picked ....
.... United States News & World Report   20
Roper, Elmo, and Harris, Louis. Whose Government Is It?
.... Saturday Review of Literature   24
Gosnell, Harold F. Do the Parties Need Help? .. Annals
    of the American Academy of Political and Social Science   27
Carleton, William G. Should Political Issues Be Sharper?
.... Yale Review   29

THE NOMINATION

Editor's Introduction 37
How Delegates Are Chosen .... Business Week   37
Stokes, Thomas L. Getting the Nomination ....
.... New York Times Magazine   38
Farley, James A. How Conventions Are Run ....
.... United States News & World Report   41
Commager, Henry Steele. What Conventions Should Do ..
.... Senior Scholastic   51
Burns, James MacGregor. A Practical Political Device ....
.... New York Times Magazine   54

Becker, Carl. Where Compromises Are Made . . . .
. . . . Yale Review 58

Kefauver, Estes, and Shalett, Sidney. Plea for a National
Primary . . . . Collier's 61

McNickle, Roma K. What Primaries Should Do . . . .
. . . . Editorial Research Reports 65

Hard, William. How the Voter Can Have His Say . . . . . .
. . . . Reader's Digest 71

The Campaign

Editor's Introduction 75

Commager, Henry Steele. Campaigns Let Off Steam . . . . . .
. . . . Senior Scholastic 75

Bone, Hugh A. Carrying the Case to the People . . Annals
of the American Academy of Political and Social Science 78

Gallup, George, and Lydgate, William A. Do Campaigns
Change Votes? . . . . Saturday Evening Post 81

Congress Is Important, Too . . . . Christian Century 90

Reston, James. Are Campaigns Too Tough? . . . .
. . . . New York Times Magazine 92

Fliegers, Serge. Do Campaigns Cost Too Much? . . . .
. . . . American Mercury 98

The Election

Editor's Introduction 108

How We Elect A President . . . .
. . . . Journal of the National Education Association 108

Krock, Arthur. Are Electors Bound in Their Votes? . . . .
. . . . New York Times 110

Dolliver, James I. History of the Electoral System . . . . . .
. . . . Vital Speeches of the Day 112

Andrews, John B. Plea for Direct Election . . . . . . Forum 117

Brown, Thomas J. Against Direct Election . . . . . . Forum 122

Becker, Carl. The Will of the People ...... Yale Review 127
Lodge, Henry Cabot, Jr. Lodge Argues For His Plan ....
.... Rotarian 131
Patman, Wright. Patman Opposes Lodge Plan .. Rotarian 137
Wechsler, Herbert. Lodge's Proposals Weighed .. Fortune 140
Ferguson, Homer. Ferguson Asks Some Questions 147
Brewer, Basil. Republican Opposition Views 150
Williams, J. Harvie. For the Coudert Proposal 155
Lea, Clarence F. Against Election by Districts 157
Wilmerding, Lucius, Jr. Two Chief Proposals Compared .. 160
Smathers, George. Senator Smathers Proposes Three Changes 165
How the Ten-Year Limit Works ....
.... United States News & World Report 168
If a President-Elect Dies ....
.... United States News & World Report 169
Wilmerding, Lucius, Jr. The Presidential Succession ......
.... Atlantic Monthly 171

APPENDIX

The Constitution 177
Public Law 771—80th Congress 179
Lodge-Gossett Plan 186
The Coudert Proposal 188
Senator Smathers' Proposal 189

BIBLIOGRAPHY 190

THE PARTY SYSTEM

EDITOR'S INTRODUCTION

The two-party system is, for better or for worse, the foundation of our present electoral setup. It is only through the machinery of the Democratic or the Republican party that the voter can give effective expression to his choice for the presidency of the United States.

In the first article of this section, a political scientist and practical politician describes the party organizations, from precinct to national level. A political "boss" contributes a frank and realistic piece on the reasons for political machines and bosses.

Another piece describes who are chosen, and why, as delegates to the national conventions that name the party candidates. Two opinion analysts report on a survey of the public attitude toward pre-election political processes which permits politicians to maintain a monopoly of these important functions.

The last two articles, both by political scientists, discuss what aid may be given to candidates for office to free them of dependence on political machines, and whether a sharper division on issues and appeals to economic groups would make for more responsible party government.

HOW POLITICAL PARTIES FUNCTION [1]

The permanent organization [of American political parties] consists of the tiers of committees that reach from top to bottom of the party hierarchy. The periodic organization includes the party primaries and conventions, which take place annually, biennially, or quadrennially, and which decide highly important questions of party policy and structure.

Once in four years, in the presidential campaigns, these party bodies achieve their greatest activity, beginning when the national committees set the time, the place, and the apportionment of the national conventions, and ending after the first Tuesday after the

[1] From "Present Party Organization and Finance," by Dean E. McHenry, professor of political science at the University of California at Los Angeles and a Democratic candidate for Congress in the 1952 elections. *Annals of the American Academy of Political and Social Science*. 283:122-6. September 1952. Reprinted by permission.

first Monday of November in the exhilaration of victory or the
despair of defeat. After the national convention has produced
the nominees, the presidential candidate makes known his choice
for national chairman, and the new national committee ratifies it
as a matter of course. The chairman, acting under the authority
of the national committee of his own choosing, manages the
party's campaign and the party national headquarters. The campaign committees—senatorial and congressional—direct campaign efforts to elect party nominees to national legislative posts.

Below the national level, all states have party state central
committees, but their composition and role vary considerably.
Some state central committees bear the principal responsibility
for conducting the campaigns of the party tickets. In other states,
leading candidates may prefer to run "lone wolf" campaigns
separate from or parallel to a general campaign under official
party committee auspices. State committeemen are chosen in a
variety of ways, by election or by appointment, and represent legislative districts, counties, or some other subdivision of the state.
They range in size from a handful in some states to more than
seven hundred in California.

Since the primary has become almost universal in the United
States, and because in many areas nomination is tantamount to
election, attention ought to be concentrated upon organizing and
financing primaries. Data on primary operations are difficult to
obtain. Official party structure plays little or no part in the nominating process in most states. The Federal corrupt-practices law
[Hatch Act] does not apply to primaries, although such application would probably be held valid in the courts. There are no
primary candidates' financial returns on file in Washington invit-
ing analysis. The most recent investigation of campaign expenditures by a House of Representatives committee showed that congressional candidates reported raising and spending more in the
1950 primaries than they did in the general election. The vast
area of activity indicated by this expenditure is not ordinarily
covered in general descriptions of party activity.

Whether it be a presidential aspirant working for pledged
delegates or a strong vote in preference primaries, or a candidate
for state or congressional office, an initial step usually is the

formation of a committee in support of the candidate. For the higher offices, such committees are often incorporated as non-profit corporations in order to free the candidate and his supporters from individual financial liability. Varying widely with state law, the purposes and objects of the corporation may be stated in terms of promoting the candidacy, cooperating with other bodies, developing interest of the electorate, receiving and spending money, suing and being sued, contracting and being contracted with, and other purposes. The candidate himself normally is not a member of the corporation and is thereby free to disclaim responsibility for the financial transactions of the entity.

The unofficial political committee, while usually free to chose its own internal organizational pattern, often develops one similar to those of official bodies. The top echelon is made up of a general chairman and perhaps a strategy committee composed of chairmen of various staff-type committees, such as finance, organization, and publicity. As in all forms of organization, especially those hastily improvised, strong personalities stand out, and when the campaign ends, someone who was never assigned a regular position may be in . . . charge of some of the most important operations.

The enthusiasms and energy of the volunteer workers rank with money in importance in building an effective campaign. In many instances, it is dislike or hate of an opposition candidate that provides the initial impetus for the volunteer to offer his services. His transformation into an effective, positive campaign worker generally depends upon the qualities of the candidate and the skill of those whose job it is to put volunteers at constructive work. Although the layers of inertia that blunt the civic consciousness of urban man may be penetrated by hate, his full usefulness after being aroused requires an affirmative cause in which he can believe.

Many experienced campaigners have noted that men and women are increasingly hard to interest in political activity. Preoccupied with his own job or family responsibilities, and absorbed by the opiate of mass entertainment reaching within the home itself, the voter demonstrates unprecedented unawareness of the necessity for widespread political participation in a democracy. . . . The voter appears to be far less informed than he was a generation ago. The proportion of real political activists is declining alarmingly. Can democracy survive with political fertility as monopolized as is reproductive capacity in a beehive?

Insufficient attention has been given in the past to the interrelationship of nation-wide campaigns with those of state and district candidates. It has been assumed rather widely that the national ticket carries along with it candidates for state and congressional office. So it does when there is a landslide victory for a presidential candidate. In given states or districts, however, the state and local candidates may save the day for the national slate. Without strong candidates for governor and senator like Adlai Stevenson and Paul H. Douglas, one could doubt President Truman's ability to carry Illinois in 1948. Great figures like Franklin D. Roosevelt carry in the wake many fellow partisans who otherwise could not have been elected. A lesser presidential candidate may have to lean heavily on state and district candidates who are relatively stronger in their own bailiwicks. . . .

Strategy of a given campaign must, of course, be determined on the basis of the fullest possible information regarding the product to be marketed—the candidate—and the circumstances under which the sale must be made, including an assessment of buyer resistance. A final election in a predominantly one-party state presents no special difficulty; the job is to get out enough partisans to maks sure that the opposition, such as it is, pulls no surprise. . . . The independent must be cultivated assiduously, for he holds the balance of power, and victory for either side will require his conversion. . . .

The objects for which campaign money is spent show little change from campaign to campaign. The House committee that studied the 1950 congressional campaign finance reported that the average candidate spent money for the following (in declining order of amount): newspaper and magazine advertising, radio and television time, salaries and expenses of campaign workers, and billboards and signs. Increasing emphasis is being placed on radio and television. Chairman McKinney of the Democratic National Committee announced [in 1952] that a million dollars of the committee's budget of $2.8 million would be spent for broadcasting and telecasting.

In examining sources of funds, legal restrictions must be taken into account. Federal law and most state laws forbid corporation contributions, but this is easily evaded by paying bonuses or other extra compensation to officers and having them contribute to campaigns. Since 1943 trade unions have been forbidden to contribute, and under the Taft-Hartley Act they are forbidden to spend union funds on political objectives. These restrictions do not apply to sums from unions' political funds that are raised through voluntary gifts. The Hatch Act restricts individual contributions to $5,000 per year to each political committee. This is evaded by contributing $5,000 each to a large number of committees.

The individual contribution from the well-to-do person remains the mainstay of party finance. Large sums are raised indirectly from the same source through high-fee dinners and advertisements in party papers and programs.

It is impossible to assess with any degree of certainty the amount of money that flows into politics from businesses and unions, despite the limits on corporate and labor union sources. Not only is the prohibitory law evaded regularly, but the government also loses tax revenue when these concerns pay printing or other bills on behalf of candidates and obscure it in their books as a business expense.

Most of the existing Federal laws relating to campaign funds are archaic and ridiculous. Sometimes they do more harm than good. For example, the $3 million limitation imposed by the Hatch Act and the $5,000 ceiling on individual contributions have induced the proliferation of political committees, which has decreased responsibility for spending. The existing maxima on spending by Senate candidates at $25,000 and by House candidates at $5,000 are so far below realistic levels that even the conscientious candidate in a large state or district finds himself referring matters of campaign finance more and more to committees that often do not report their expenditures under Federal and state law.

Ceilings on expenditures are unworkable under present enforcement provisions. The honest step is to repeal all limitations on amounts, as California did recently. The main purpose of our corrupt-practices law should be to turn the light of publicity on spending. Consequently, primary emphasis ought to be placed on getting full reports and fixing responsibility for spending. The outstanding weakness of our law can be corrected only when expenditures on behalf of a candidate can be made legally only by that candidate or his appointed agent.

WHY MACHINES AND BOSSES? [2]

I have been chairman of the Democratic Executive Committee of Bronx County for a quarter century. In order to remain in that position, I must always have the committee votes to support me. My control is entirely dependent upon this support. If a majority of the committee decided they no longer wanted me, they could call a meeting tomorrow and supplant me. But during my entire service as chairman, there has never been any serious threat. There has been occasional scattered opposition, but never any real danger.

How do I maintain the majority support of the Executive Committee? To begin with, I always see to it that the key party workers have exempt positions [i.e., not subject to civil service regulations], if they want them. Some of the salaries are small (particularly those given to women). They run from $2,500 to $5,000, with only one at $10,000. Still, to use the political parlance, all the district leaders have been "taken care of" during my entire term as county leader. In New York County, by contrast, there have been many changes among the district leaders during the same period—because they were not put in exempt positions. The biggest turnover came about when the Democrats lost the county in the Fusion heyday. Bronx County is the only county within the city [New York] that has never been defeated either for county or for borough offices.

    [2] From "Bosses and Machines," by Edward J. Flynn, chairman of the Democratic Executive Committee of Bronx County, N.Y. *Atlantic Monthly.* 179:34-40. May 1947. Reprinted by permission.

The families also—sons, daughters, husbands, wives—of the district leaders are taken care of in some way or other. Sometimes they are given exempt positions, and sometimes they get help from us in the line of civil service promotion. It is rather difficult to say if this is the real reason why I have had their support down through the years, but I cannot deny that it has been extremely important to my remaining as leader.

There is one other important factor in retaining the support of the Executive Committee, and although it has never been put to test, I am confident that it could be with perfect safety. I have the final word about who should be appointed to positions which control exempt jobs. The county committeemen who select the executive members know this. Also, it is inevitable that during these years of my leadership I have come to know these committeemen well, and they in turn to know me. I feel sure that should I express to them a desire to have a district leader removed, a new leader would be selected immediately. Thus not only my long association with the party, but my absolute control of exempt positions, is a powerful influence in my control.

The importance of this business of patronage in the success of a party and a leader may be seen by studying the strengthening of the Democratic party during Roosevelt's terms as governor of New York and his first terms in the White House. Because he paid attention to his leaders and made the party appointments they recommended (always after previously investigating the candidate's abilities), Roosevelt built up the greatest vote-getting machine, both state and Federal, that has ever been known. When he began to accept the recommendations of the New Dealers of "nonpolitical" appointments, there was a falling away of his vote-getting ability. However, by that time Roosevelt's name had such magic that he was able, notwithstanding, to maintain his leadership. . . .

Victory is easier for the organization than for the insurgent. The organization at all times has its own personnel in each small unit. An insurgent who questions the decisions of the machine must first place a man and woman captain in every election district. This is not an easy task. It is difficult to build up in two or three months what it has taken the organization years to achieve. Furthermore, under a good administration, it is not easy to find enough people who will disagree with the machine.

At various times, candidates for the legislature have challenged the nominees of the organization. There have been primary fights. But in every instance, the organization has won, because all its forces could be centered in the troublesome district. The result has been that the insurgent not only was defeated, but overwhelmingly so.

Once a person who has been a member of the organization turns against it in a primary election, he is forever barred from any political preferment. Since most people who feel like fighting the organization have hopes for political advancement, the assignment to organization Coventry makes their political futures dubious, to say the least. . . .

A political leader or "boss," however, must not only be able to pick his men, but he must be able to "guess right." During my leadership, I have been lucky enough to do this in many political situations. . . .

All these things together have helped to build my strength as a leader. My district leaders realize that I have usually guessed right. It has put the Bronx organization in the forefront in various campaigns, and my leaders have taken pride in the fact that because of my friendship with Roosevelt I have become a national figure in the Democratic party.

The impression of secrecy which seems to veil the position of political boss exists for no other reason than that the idea has been handed down from one political generation to another. Most of the appearance of secrecy arises from the fact that the leader himself cannot make up his mind what course to pursue— or more often, because it is not propitious to announce his decision at the precise moment the newspapers clamor for it.

Political skill is mostly built on proper timing. The correct time to announce a candidacy or the support of a particular candidate is as important as the announcement itself. If it is badly timed, the whole effect can be lost. In this connection, Roosevelt often resorted to the "trial balloon"—that is, letting someone other than himself make a statement to see how it would be received by the public. If the time was not right, the statement would be critized severely. If it was well received, Roosevelt would step in and "carry the ball." I myself have never been completely convinced that this is a good thing to do, but I am considerably in the minority in that opinion.

Should a man announce his candidacy too far in advance of a convention or primary, he can easily kill himself off through the opposition which will tend to develop and crystallize. Therefore, in practical politics an announcement is delayed as long as practicable, to prevent such a situation. It is usually thoroughly understood between a candidate and a leader just what the leader intends to do, and the leader very seldom lets the cat out of the bag until it is absolutely necessary to do so. . . .

As long as we have a two-party system of government, we shall have machines. Whether they will be good or bad depends upon the interest of citizens in their party government, and upon whether that interest is just as strong and unflagging as their interest in their local, state and Federal governments.

The reason more people do not accept the inevitability of machine politics is that whenever they think of machines and bosses, they seem to think only of the successful ones. In every county in New York City there is and always has been a Republican machine. To be sure, they call themselves "organizations," but they are as truly machines as their Democratic counterparts in every respect save that of success at the polls. The nominations for the various offices in the Republican party are dictated by the Republican county leaders, who are, of course, the Republican county bosses. . . .

This is equally true throughout the United States. In practically every city and every state, there are a Republican machine and a Democratic machine, and there is always one man who is the boss of the machine. The final responsibility for nominations is wholly in his hands. Thus, when you condemn the "boss system" you condemn both major parties and indeed all political parties, because all operate in exactly the same way.

This system is a direct result of the election laws not only in the state of New York but in every state of the Union. The election laws provide the method under which parties are organized. The same laws that apply to the Democratic party apply to the Republican party.

If this is true, then what can be done and what should be done? One must work with the tools at hand. If a machine is bad, it can be reformed only by the members of the party concerned. Many people criticize government—and then announce that they are not affiliated with either of the major parties. This is ridiculous. They can never hope, through unorganized mass, to accomplish anything. If they wish to cure a situation, they must do it through the machinery that is set up by the election laws.

I do not want to minimize how difficult a job this is. It is difficult because in a successful machine the leaders have so well fortified themselves that it takes time to upset them. It cannot be done in a year. In some cases, it cannot be done for many years. But if the start is made, eventually the vicious element in an organization can be removed. Those who have the courage and persistence to survive early discouragements win out in the end. . . .

There is no use periodically electing "Fusion" or "Good Government" candidates. They will either stay in power a short time, or they will set up their own machines, or—what is far more likely—they will merge back into one or the other of the two major parties. The Republican and Democratic parties have survived a good many "reform" movements in the form of third parties, the one over a period of ninety years, the other over a period of nearly a century and a half. Third-party movements have never succeeded nationally. They have succeeded about once in fifty times in the states. They have succeeded, all too briefly, about once in twenty times in the cities. These figures speak for themselves.

If we are to have uniformly good government, local, state, and national, I am afraid a lot of men and women will have to get down off their high horses and grub around in practical politics as active members of a party. I wish we had in our school systems required courses of training in citizenship which would send forth graduates by the hundreds of thousands who would assume such responsibilities as readily and naturally as they assume the responsibility of earning a living. So far as I can see, the emphasis in whatever practical politics is taught is placed upon elections, rather than primaries. The so-called "independent" voter is all but deified, when he ought to be condemned as a shirker.

Waiting until after the candidates are nominated is waiting until you have missed the boat. Whatever is to be done must be done before the nominations are made. There is no machine—I do not care how powerful and well entrenched it appears to be— that would dare to nominate a candidate for office it knew its own people did not want. Many poor candidates are named because of the fact that the great majority of the members of his party would take no interest in the primary election anyway. Bosses get away with a good deal by default—your default.

Today much criticism is being leveled at the Political Action Committee [of the Congress of Industrial Organizations] because of the fact that it is taking an active part in the primaries of the Republican and Democratic parties, seeking to have named on both sides candidates who are friendly to PAC—which is to say, to organized labor. PAC has become a very potent factor in national politics. In states like New York, Pennsylvania, New Jersey, Illinois, Massachusetts, and some border states, its intensive work undoubtedly helped in the election of President Roosevelt in 1940 and 1944.

It is significant, I think, for the student of politics that PAC did not set out to form a third party and thus far has resisted the temptation to do so on a national scale. The tactics are fundamentally the same as those of people who choose to work with one of the older parties, in that the aim is to influence the selection of candidates before the choice has narrowed to two. That the results are sometimes more meager than those obtained by Republican and Democratic "regulars," at least in New York City, has been indicated in several recent elections there. . . . To be successful at the polls, PAC usually has to make common cause with one or the other of the old-line parties and vote for its candidates. . . .

If the citizens whose interests are different from or broader than those championed by PAC would take as much pains to protect those interests as labor is taking to protect its interests, the story might be an entirely different one. Certainly there is no point in condemning PAC-endorsed candidates because of their obligation to organized labor. Unfortunately, however, the citizen with broad interests is rarely a party worker, or even an active citizen. Why, therefore, should he be surprised that more "independent" candidates are not elected to office? It would be a fine thing if all officeholders felt under obligation to all types of citizens, and hence based their judgments on the rule of the greatest long-term good for the greatest number. But we shall never reach that Utopia unless or until all the citizens resolve to work 365 days a year at being citizens.

There, then, is the machine and its boss. While bosses are inevitable, under our system of government, bad bosses are not. For, in the last analysis, the real boss is you.

HOW CANDIDATES ARE PICKED [3]

Politicians, not voters, decide who gets a chance to run for President of the United States. The voters, every four years, as in 1952, only get a chance to decide which man, of those selected by the politicians, they prefer for the job.

The show that candidates put on for the public, prior to the national conventions, is mere shadowboxing. They hope, by attracting popular support, to win the attention of the few politicians who finally do the choosing. . . .

All of this raises a question about how a presidential candidate really is chosen and how a President finally is elected.

In the whole process, from the . . . [conventions or primaries] to the balloting . . . and on to the final choice of a President in the electoral college, the voter gets no chance to vote directly for or against any individual for President. The part that is played by the voter is indirect throughout.

[3] From "How a President Is Chosen." *United States News & World Report,* an independent weekly news magazine on national and international affairs published at Washington, D.C. 32:19-21. February 1, 1952. Copyright 1952, United States News Publishing Corporation. Reprinted by permission.

In the end, presidential electors, if they wish, can vote against the expressed desires of the voters in their state. On two or three occasions individual electors have done so.

It is in the choice of party candidates for the presidency, however, that the voters' role is least decisive and that of the politicians most decisive.

The candidates for President are named in party conventions. . . . Here delegates from all the states will decide among the claims of the candidates of the two parties and pick presidential candidates. But the delegates who do the choosing either are politicians themselves or are speaking for the politicians. This makes it important for voters to understand how delegates are selected and what power they have.

Almost half of the delegates to national conventions are chosen by the politicians through a state convention system. In thirty-two of the forty-eight states, the delegates are picked by party machinery that reaches down to the precincts. These thirty-two states furnish more than 575 of the almost 1,200 delegates in each party.

And most of these 575 delegates are hand-picked by the politicians in the thirty-two states, operating through a maze of state and district and county committees that the parties have created to reach the voters. Ordinarily, these committees operate in presenting candidates to the voters. But, in presidential election years, they act for the voters in choosing a candidate.

This network of committees reaches from Washington into virtually every important county in the nation. At the middle are the national committees of the two parties. These have two members from each state. Next are the state committees, with members from counties or congressional districts. Third link is the county or congressional-district committee. At the outer edge of the network, in some cases, are town and election-district committees. Everywhere, working politicians hold the positions of power.

It is this mechanism, controlled at all the sensitive spots by working party men, that handles the selection of presidential candidates. The voter has little to say about it, although the politicians are alert to catch his reaction to the potential candidates. The politicians want candidates who can win.

At the top of the organizations, the national committees set the dates and places for the national conventions. They decide how many delegates each state may send to these conventions. There are two politicians from each state on the national committee, and each of these would be an important dispenser of patronage if his party's candidate should win the presidency. . . .

Closely tied with the work of the national committees in most states are the state committees of the two parties. . . . In most of the thiry-two convention states a very small number of men—from one to five—pick most of the delegates.

There is a routine procedure. Towns and election districts pick delegates to county or district conventions. Some states hold mass meetings, which citizens usually leave in the hands of the politicians. Often the members of city and county committees simply pick the delegates without the formality of such meetings. And, when meetings are held, few citizens show up. The politicians go because that is their business.

County and district conventions pick the delegates to state conventions. Here, again, the local political leaders dominate. These usually have a tie-in with a senator, a governor, the state chairman, or the state's national committeeman. And many of the delegates to the state convention are hand-picked. This permits the key party figures in the state to rule the convention.

There are from three to six men in key party spots in each state. If these men are working together, they can control a state convention. Often, one or two important men can swing a state convention into line.

When presidential candidates claim delegate votes before state conventions are held, they base these claims on friendship with important men in the states. They think these men will be able to control the state meetings. But there always are at least two factions in each party in every state, and conventions can get out of hand. . . .

In the final analysis, however, a hundred men will dominate the choice of the 575 delegates from the thirty-two states that use the convention system. They work from the state level, at the top, using jobs, patronage, favors, or the hope of them, to keep their supporters.

Even in the sixteen states in which the voters choose their 600 delegates in party primaries, the hold that the voters have over those delegates is very loose. In fourteen of those states the delegates are free to quit the candidate picked by the voters whenever they see fit. Only in New Hampshire and Wisconsin are they bound by law to stay with the candidate approved by their voters. In New Hampshire, they must vote for this candidate as long as his name is before the national convention. In Wisconsin, they must stick to him as long as he gets 10 per cent of the convention vote.

After preliminary skirmishes in the national convention, most delegates are free to switch to whatever candidates they wish. And unless one of the candidates goes into a convention with such an overwhelming lead that he wins on an early ballot, this puts the final selection into the hands of a few powerful state leaders. From twelve to forty men might have the privilege of picking a presidential candidate.

Once the conventions are over, the politicians go home and draw up their lists of presidential electors, if this job has not already been done by the state conventions. Prominent local politicians and their substantial backers go on these lists. No Federal officeholders may be included. This is forbidden by the Constitution.

All through the campaign, the voters hear speeches by contending candidates. The personalities of the presidential nominees are portrayed in a hundred different ways.

But, when the voters go into the polling booths . . . [in] November . . . they . . . vote for a slate of electors the politicians have chosen. . . . They . . . choose between slates of electors designated by names of parties or candidates, depending on state law.

Even here, the politicians have not finished. The presidential electors must meet in the states and cast their votes. These must be sent to Washington and opened in a formal, joint session of Congress, and tallied.

Usually, the electors vote as their state did. But they are not bound by law to do so. One Democratic elector in Tennessee refused in 1948 to vote for Mr. Truman. There is at least one other such case in history.

If no candidate has a majority of the electoral votes, the three top names are submitted to the House of Representatives, where a majority of the states is required for a choice. Here each state must vote as a unit, and the politicians wrangle their way to a decision.

WHOSE GOVERNMENT IS IT? [4]

Politically speaking, the United States might well be described as a dog wagged by a tail. In a very real sense we are a nation of minority rule, because a majority of our people abstain from politics, abdicating in favor of a few professional politicians and their coteries of insiders and hangers-on.

It isn't that people don't believe in the process of free elections. It is simply that they surrender the process to the politicians and party hacks through default. Yet in a series of surveys studying this problem the writers have found that the American people cherish the right to vote more than any other liberty. When put to a choice, more people would rather give up such inviolate rights as their freedom of speech, assembly, and religion than abandon free elections. Unfortunately, many of the same people who find the right to vote so precious have never been inside a polling booth. For example, just last November the elections used up thousands of lines of newsprint, pushed virtually everything else off the front pages, and caused a multitude of personal arguments. But for all the sound and fury, some 56 per cent of the voters stayed at home on election day. Just over 42 million out of some 95 million eligibles took the trouble to vote.

This must have been a strange sight to people in Western Europe, for since their liberation in 1945 between 70 and 95

[4] From "Crime, Reform & the Voter," by Elmo Roper and Louis Harris, public opinion analysts. *Saturday Review of Literature.* 34:7-9+. April 7, 1951. Reprinted by permission.

per cent of their eligible voters have turned out. Here in America, however, such lethargy at the polls is old hat. At least four out of every ten people who are over twenty-one years of age simply have never taken the trouble to vote. Depending on the year, between 35 and 50 per cent of the people always decide what kind of a government we will have here. The rest of the population, largely by self-choice, in effect disenfranchises itself.

As deplorable as this state of political affairs might be, however, it is also true that more people participate in voting than in any other part of the political process. And, as any successful officeholder will testify, while the vote may be crucial, it is neither the end-all nor the beginning of the political process. . . .

Last year [1950], in a study sponsored by the Standard Oil Company (New Jersey), we decided we would take a closer look at political activity in this country and measure the extent to which people do take part in the political process.

After a good deal of probing into the political process, we came up with what we believe are six key facets of political activity. . . .

Voting: Some 75 per cent of our cross section claimed they had voted once or more in the past four years; 47 per cent three times or more; and 21 per cent five times or more. We have good evidence to indicate that this is more a wishful than an accurate estimate.

Belonging to organizations: Only 31 per cent report that they belong to organizations which take stands on public issues, and another 7 per cent say they belong to two or more such groups. . . .

Discussing public issues with others: Some 21 per cent of the people say they discuss public issues frequently and take at least an equal share in the conversation, while only 6 per cent say they try to do some "missionary" work in the frequent discussions they have on the state of the nation. Either the people are much too busy with their own private affairs, or perhaps they simply aren't overly impressed with the meaning and significance of the "great debates" which were supposed to have been rocking the nation in recent years.

Writing or talking to a public official: Only 13 per cent report they have written a letter or talked with a congressman or other public official on a public issue within the past year; and another 7 per cent say they wrote or spoke to the representative two or more times. We have heard a good deal in the past about the "floods" of mail which have descended on Congress. And while it doesn't take much, perhaps, to inundate a congressman's overworked office, a singularly small number of Americans appear to have taken the trouble to register their thoughts with their elected representatives.

Worked in a political campaign: Some 11 per cent of the people report they have worked for the election of a political candidate in the last four years. A traditional cry of the "outs" in politics is that the machine is too well entrenched, too powerful to buck. If that is so, then the machines must have their entire army manning the front lines, with very thin or non-existent reserves. For 11 per cent—when divided between two major parties and spread across the country—doesn't add up to what might be called a comprehensive network of political organizations.

Contributed money to a campaign: A total of 7 per cent of the people say that they gave some money to a party or a candidate in the past four years. Last fall, it will be recalled, literally millions of dollars were reported to have been built up in political war chests. If that was so, then rarely have so few contributed so much as have the people who contribute to political campaigns.

These percentages of people who do these various political deeds are, of course, based simply on what people *say* they have done. If there is a bias in any direction, it is fairly certain to be on the inflationary side. People usually claim to have done more than they actually did. If that reasoning is sound, then we are forced to conclude that to call even 10 per cent of the American people politically active animals is exaggeration of sorts and undoubtedly a generous statement. . . .

It is evident that with fewer than half the people voting and with hardly more than 10 per cent of the people engaging in active politics, the question of who these people are politically is an important one. . . .

In the population as a whole, the Democrats outnumber the Republicans by a wide margin—some 16 percentage points. However, among the politically very active people, the Republicans reverse the trend and hold a 4 percentage point lead. In abbreviated form, these over-all figures illustrate a major finding of our study: the Republicans overcome the handicap of having fewer party followers by having more of almost everything that counts politically. . . . Republicans tend to contribute money, work in campaigns, belong to more organizations, communicate with public officials and discuss issues more frequently than do Democrats. Clearly the Republicans put more time and effort into their politics than do Democrats.

But the sharpest difference between the political activity patterns of the two parties lies in the voting behavior of their members. Our survey indicated the Republicans have brought out 61 per cent of their potential voters at least once over the past four years, while the Democrats have been able to get only 42 per cent of their party followers out to the polls this often. . . .

Perhaps more of the people would vote if a greater number of people engaged in political activity. It might well be that with scarcely more than 10 per cent of the people in the "very active" group we cannot hope for a larger turnout than 50 per cent.

When close to half the people don't vote, we get representatives of but part of the people. When hardly more than 10 per cent of the people take the trouble to influence the choice of the candidates and less than 20 per cent try to influence officials, once they are elected to office, the democratic process in America can hardly be called a model of functioning self-rule.

DO THE PARTIES NEED HELP? [5]

In the United States the political parties are still the backbone of the vote-getting machinery. The parties raise the funds and recruit workers to bring the voters to the polls. The Kefauver and other investigations have shown that the parties in the great

[5] From "Participation in the Forthcoming Election," by Harold F. Gosnell, adjunct professor of political science, American University, Washington, D.C. *Annals of the American Academy of Political and Social Science.* 283:156-60. September 1952. Reprinted by permission.

urban centers find it easier to obtain funds from the underworld than from other groups. Party precinct workers expect rewards in the form of political patronage and special favors. The citizens in the lower income groups who wish to enter politics are faced with unpleasant choices. If they do not line up with the party machines, their chances of success are small. If they become members of the party organization, their voices are silenced on many reform issues.

Should the government lighten the burden of the parties in mobilizing the electorate? In what ways might the government aid candidates without interfering with freedom of choice?

Some forty years ago it was proposed in the United States that the government itself undertake to give financial aid to candidates for elective office. Except for a limited amount of free radio time, little has been done to implement such a proposal in this country.

In postwar Japan, however, a full and logical application of the government's responsibility to promote freedom of candidacy has been made. With the elimination of the former militarist and expansionist leaders, it was necessary to encourage the participation in politics of those who were without organization support and who lacked the funds necessary to conduct a modern election campaign. It was assumed that in a democracy all persons, regardless of means or status, should be accorded equal opportunity in seeking public office.

For the 1947 elections a National Election Administration Commission was established, with nine members named by the National Diet. This commission's duties included the administration of the appropriation which paid subsidies to candidates for the conduct of their campaigns. The subsidies were in the form of gasoline ration coupons, free passes on public transportation facilities, free radio time, payment for newspaper advertisements, space in the election gazette, free postage, a limited supply of free paper, and an opportunity to take part in the free competitive speech meetings.

Judging by the size of the polls, the Japanese election laws have been quite successful. In 1947 some 68 per cent of the eligible vote was cast; in 1949 it rose to 74 per cent, and in 1950 to 80 per cent.

A corollary of the limited subsidy plan in Japan has been a limit on the total amount of money that each candidate can spend on his own account. According to American standards, a low limit is applied.

The Japanese laws have brought about a wider participation in running for elective office. In the 1947 elections a considerable number of farmers, teachers, labor leaders, journalists, doctors, and housewives were elected to the House of Representatives.

Compulsory voting is an older device which has been used by a number of European and other countries to see that the voters perform their duties on election day. It has been particularly successful in Australia.

If compulsory voting were to be used in the United States, it would mean that the registration and voting laws would have to be strengthened and made more nearly uniform, and that voting administration would have to be centralized. The most ignorant citizens would probably cast blank ballots, but they would be under pressure to inform themselves and make the most intelligent choices that they could. Compulsory voting would probably help the Democrats more than the Republicans under present circumstances. As far as the tone of politics is concerned, compulsory voting would be an improvement, since it would reduce the need for large political organizations, large campaign funds, and patronage rewards for party canvassers who round up voters. The parties would have to concentrate on winning the support of the voters, not merely bringing out the faithful.

SHOULD PARTY ISSUES BE SHARPER? [6]

In striking fashion the presidential election of 1952 has once more revealed how faint and wavering is the line that differentiates the Republican and Democratic parties. A more clear-cut realignment of American parties may be slowly taking place, particularly in the prairie corn and wheat states and in the South,

[6] From "A More Responsible Party System?" by William G. Carleton, professor of political science, University of Florida. *Yale Review*. 42, no3:410-27. Spring [March] 1953. Reprinted by permission.

and this may have decisive consequences for the future. Today, however, as the campaign and election revealed, our parties are still pretty much as they have always been. The question arises whether this is or is not a good thing for the welfare of the nation.

American politics have always been nonideological. The American two-party system has consistently defied clear-cut and logical divisions. Both major parties are broad and inclusive. Since factions within the parties commonly are tantamount to several separate parties, at any given time there are in fact not two but five or six separate parties in the state legislatures and in Congress. This has been true all through American history, not just since . . . [1948], although the Dixiecrat-Republican alliance since that date has made this situation better known.

The history of legislation of any session of Congress is the story of how the factions within the parties align, realign, interweave and crisscross. All sorts of bipartisan combinations are made to pass and to obstruct legislation. In times of crisis and change, the bipartisan combinations to stop legislation are more numerous, as during the closing years of the Wilson Administration and during the Roosevelt Administration after 1938. As Samuel Lubell has suggested recently, the decisive power conflicts of any given era are largely determined by the conflicts and compromises of the factions inside the normally majority party of that era. . . .

The [1952] election's reaffirmation of the traditional American system of nonideological politics is all the more significant because of recent tendencies towards a realignment of our two major parties on more sharply drawn lines. There has been a tendency for American politics to become less sectional, less decentralized, less amorphous. . . .

In short, a two-party system has been developing in the corn and wheat states and in the South, although in the South this development has been more gradual and less direct. Before the election all of this seemed to indicate that our parties were on the way to becoming more clearly differentiated, more class and group conscious, more national, more centralized. . . .

Perhaps most Americans, impressed by the frenetic election oratory of campaign years, do not fully realize to what degree American politics are the politics of consensus, of genuine agreement on essentials by both the major parties. The wide variety of groups inside each party produces internal contradictions out of which emerge compromises and basic similarities of outlook. Within our major parties extreme groups and positions are more than counterbalanced by the more numerous moderate groups which temper extremism. Crypto-Communists are kept in check inside the Democratic party (all the more, since the Wallace third-party fiasco), and crypto-Fascists have been kept in check within the Republican party. If the internal balancing of interests is unsatisfactory, there are always groups within the party ready to cooperate with the other party to check their own party. Thus the Republican party is always being forced to the center or to a little right of center; likewise the Democratic party is forced to the center or to a little left of center. . . .

Only in the United States has there been enough consensus among the major parties for all of them to claim relationship to the same seers and prophets. . . .

In America, differences are adjusted within the parties and between the parties; in Europe's multiple-party system extreme groups rise to prominence and power more easily, exercise greater influence, are not held in leash by intraparty balancing. There the significant adjustments have to be made among the parties and not within them. The differences are too clearly perceived; the way to compromise is rendered difficult. In America, in time of great change, both parties contribute to the change; when change is slowed down, both parties unite to slow it down.

Moreover, the concrete policy pursued by any administration anywhere consists of an aggregate of somewhat inconsistent parts; ideological parties can enjoy the luxury of intellectually consistent doctrines, but actual administrations cannot. Is it not better to demand that the voter deal with some of the ambiguities inherent in all broad domestic and foreign policies than for a national legislature (like the French) to have the whole burden of coping with them? True, American parties are even more ambiguous than the policies evolved by an administration, but these very ambiguities often allow for a certain amount of play for leadership which ideological parties do not.

However, in recent years, critics have arisen to challenge America's traditional party system and to emphasize its short-comings and dangers. For the most part they have been admirers of the centralized British parties, or they have been people tending to left-wing views, concerned with getting party machinery that will respond more rapidly to changing conditions. They have pointed out that in a democratic society parties must present issues in a clearcut way in order to get accurate popular verdicts, that parties must be united and centralized in order to be effectively responsive to popular verdicts. They say that events move more rapidly than in the past, that parties which are not prepared to make positive decisions with dispatch are likely to be powerless in the face of great crisis. If popular verdicts repeatedly miscarry, if confusion and frustration continue, if parties are inadequate to face crises, then, these critics say, we may be confronted with one or several of the following developments: an unhealthy overtaxing of the presidential office, even dictatorship; the movement of the American people towards the extreme right or the extreme left; even abject national failure in an hour of supreme testing.

In short, a party system which in less rapidly moving and less perilous days was noted for its moderation may in the crisis years of the mid-twentieth century actually be productive of extremism, actually may destroy the democratic process itself. Contemporary democratic institutions must be rendered flexible, responsible and capable of making rapid adjustments to change, or die, it is argued. . . .

The Committee on Political Parties of the American Political Science Association in 1950 made an important report which came out boldly for structural changes in our political and governmental system designed to nationalize, centralize, and differentiate more clearly the two major parties.

The report is a careful and elaborate attempt to draw up a table of organization for more responsible and better disciplined parties. It calls for smaller, more representative, and more vigorous national conventions, though it looks to a time when a direct primary may be a feasible and desirable means of nominating presidential and vice-presidential candidates. The report also calls for a national council and a party cabinet in each party. It conscientiously specifies what each of the groups should do and who their members should be, with the general objective of providing an organization that can formulate a consistent policy and implement it by some control over legislative programs, the distribution of party funds, and—in time, perhaps—the choice of candidates.

The report would also replace the present leadership committees in Congress (Rules Committee, Steering Committee, Committee on Committees, etc.) with party leadership committees. Congressional committee chairmanships would not be awarded solely on a seniority basis; convinced party loyalty and personal competence would also be considerations for selection. The majority party would have representation on the congressional committees well above the party's ratio in the House or Senate itself, for the present method of having about as many committee positions for the minority as for the majority gives individual members of the majority party the balance of power and invites chaos, according to the report. The report also recommends that the present cloture rule of the Senate be discarded for a majority cloture on all matters before that body. . . .

The report is remarkable in several respects. For one thing it contains no adequate acknowledgment that the whole tenor of the committee's recommendations runs counter to America's dominant political tradition of decentralized parties. Not even lip service is paid to the achievements of the conventional American party system to date. Therefore the stupendous difficulties in the way of these innovations are drastically minimized.

For another thing, the report ignores the actual realignments taking place in the corn and wheat states and in the South. The report confines itself to structural and mechanical changes in party procedures; the economic and social forces at work to produce changes in the substantive nature of our parties are passed over. And yet if these great structural and mechanical changes in America's party system are to take place, they are more likely to come after the substantive realignments, not before them. . . .

Some of the recommendations of the report might in practice actually lead to a strengthening of the traditional system rather than to the development of a more centralized system, that is, unless the substantive realignment of parties preceded the structural changes. For instance, placing large numbers of the conventional type of national committeemen, state chairmen and congressional leaders in such strategic places as a more powerful national convention, party council and party cabinet might check the one centralizing agency we now have, the presidency, and make even more influential the local, sectional, and pressure-group interests too often represented by national committeemen, state chairman, and congressional leaders.

Again, the instituting of national primaries to nominate the President and Vice President, a proposal which has already caught the popular fancy, without at the same time redrawing congressional districts of approximately equal population, a proposal infinitely difficult to accomplish, probably would further separate the President and Congress and accentuate the stalemate between executive and legislature. For national primaries would produce presidents even more responsible to national and urban interests, but such presidents would be confronted by the same rurally-weighted Congress as we have today, unless Congress were made more representative of the cities than it is now. In short, the time lag between accomplishing the various structural reforms might actually make our parties more irresponsible than they are now. . . .

There is, then, a running debate between two schools of thought on the worth of our traditional party system. One school defends it as a positive good, the other attacks it as inadequate to the needs of our age. The traditionalists have American history and habit on their side; they also realize the tremendous difficulties involved in change. Undoubtedly those who favor more clearly differentiated and centralized parties are prophetic of some future trends already discernible.

Have we reached that crisis in American affairs which the critics of our present two-party system feared, that crisis we cannot adequately meet because of the inadequacy of our party system? American foreign policy, formulated by the President, often is emasculated in Congress, even in a Congress in which the President's party has a nominal majority. The failure of our Point Four program to win anything like the support required for effectiveness is but one illustration of this failure.

Had the Democratic party in 1945 been a more clearcut leftist party, it undoubtedly would have been in a better position to cooperate with the triumphant British Labor Party in a policy of far-flung constructive social politics in Europe and Asia designed to win the masses to an Anglo-American foreign policy, a policy nearer to what a leader like Nehru would approve. People for generations will debate whether such a policy would have been more effective, whether it would have prevented the cold war or prevented the current armaments race from reaching the proportions it has now reached. But by 1945 social and economic forces had not yet converged to produce such a leftist party in the United States, nor have they done so yet. Today, in 1953, the world crisis has deepened and Americans are much more frightened than they were in 1945.

In the coming struggle to save America's heritage of freedom, it is not too much to say that the traditional party system in America, the system which does not divide people along ideological lines and which keeps lovers of freedom in both parties, is America's best bulwark against totalitarianism. Today it is well that both parties have within themselves liberals, middle-of-the-roaders, and conservatives bred in the humane tradition who are willing to fight within their parties to curb the totalitarians in their midst.

Clear-cut party divisions always tend to become ideological and totalitarian. This is true everywhere, particularly today, even in countries long accustomed to ideological parties; and it would be specially true of America, where parties based on ideological cleavage would be new and would emerge for the first time in the current period of mass fear. As long as a crisis psychology exists, it might be well not to push too rapidly the underlying tendencies which are at work to give us, ultimately, more clearly differentiated parties. Attempts to do so today are likely to frighten Americans still more and to encourage the kind of ideological division which even the sponsors of more clearly differentiated parties themselves want to avoid at all cost: a party cleavage with totalitarians in one party and nontotalitarians in the other.

In this age of crisis, America's traditional party system, which blurs and softens the issues and tensions, may do more than any other single element in American civilization for America's heritage of freedom.

THE NOMINATION

EDITOR'S INTRODUCTION

The national party conventions have the final say in nominating candidates for the presidency. The bases on which delegates to these conventions are allocated are outlined in the first article of this section. Next, a veteran Washington columnist relates what a complicated process it is, in practice, to get a party's nomination.

James A. Farley, who managed Franklin D. Roosevelt's first two campaigns, tells in a practical politician's words, just how conventions are run. A professor of history discusses what conventions, idealistically, ought to do. A political scientist defends the "smoke-filled room" as a practical device for getting things done and suggests some improvements in the management of conventions. Another historian holds a brief for conventions as a means of settling issues within parties before elections, instead of by horse-trading between parties after elections, as the French attempt to do.

A one-time presidential candidate offers a proposal for a national primary to determine the popular choices for presidential candidates. The following article analyzes the results of the primary system where it is used in this country and its merits as a gauge of candidates' popularity and as a means of electing convention delegates. Nineteen states now have primaries, and in sixteen of these national party convention delegates are elected in the primaries. (Any apparent discrepancies regarding primaries in the articles in this section are due to differences in the types of primaries referred to by the authors.) Finally, a political writer points out how a voter may participate directly in the pre-election phases of the political process.

HOW DELEGATES ARE CHOSEN [1]

Delegates to the national convention are selected in one of two ways, depending on the state: (1) They may be elected by direct vote in the presidential primaries, or (2) they may be chosen by state conventions of the party. The state conventions are usually under tight control by local party organizations.

[1] From "Convention Delegates: How Tight Are They Tied?" *Business Week*. p24-6. January 26, 1952. Reprinted by permission.

Some states use both methods of selecting delegates. Illinois elects fifty district delegates by primary and names ten delegates at large at the state convention. New York elects eighty-six district delegates in the primary and ten delegates at large at the state convention. In Minnesota, eighteen district delegates plus seven delegates at large come out of the primary; three delegates at large are chosen at the state convention.

Where there is a state convention, it may give the delegates their voting instructions, at least for the first ballot. Votes on later ballots are decided by caucus at the national convention.

Delegates from the primary states generally have more freedom to switch their votes. Only two states, Wisconsin and Minnesota [and now New Hampshire], pin their delegates down by law to support primary winners for fixed periods. Only four other primary states pledge delegates to any degree. And here the candidate has no assurance that his delegates will stick after the second or third ballot.

On the other hand, delegates from the convention states are more likely to switch in a body. They are under tighter control by state leaders and are apt to fall in line when a leader makes a deal to switch to a more promising candidate.

The practical politics of it is that delegates stay with their candidate as long as it appears they have a chance of piling up the 603 votes necessary to win. But there is nothing legally binding about this loyalty. The moment there is a stampede to a candidate, all commitments go overboard.

GETTING THE NOMINATION [2]

What vestige of democracy is there in the system of choosing delegates [to political conventions] by popular election in only seventeen of forty-eight states? Many of these primaries are dominated by the "organization vote" because of eligibility requirements or complicated procedures for handling write-in votes.

    [2] From "Getting Nominated Is an Intricate Business, by Thomas L. Stokes, Washington political columnist. New York *Times Magazine*. p9+. April 20, 1952. Reprinted by permission.

The democratic process is discounted further by the fact that only a minority of such delegates run pledged to any particular candidate and, even where they are pledged, the commitment is loose and can be abandoned easily and fairly early.

Only seven primary states have clear-cut preferential systems in which the names of the candidates are carried separately on the ballot. There is no compulsion, except in the case of Oregon, for the delegates to follow the outcome of these state-wide "popularity contests." There is no compulsion, either, for candidates to enter any of the presidential primaries, so that the voter may not have a fair chance to express a clear choice. Candidates often pick and choose their spots—according to local conditions—further thwarting the people and confusing the interpretation of popular trends.

In the thirty-one states [see introduction to this section—Ed.] where primaries do not prevail the delegates are generally selected by convention, and here the influence of bosses and local leaders is predominant. Selection of such delegates is often merely a matter of "ratification," sometimes after *pro forma* choosing at county or district conventions. Often the delegates are hand-picked with the idea of supporting one or another candidate, or for their docility when it comes to trading off delegates in the convention itself. . . .

An "open" convention . . . often means one open to bargaining by the bosses in which the people have little impact either. "Competition" produced the 1920 deadlock in the Republican convention which was only resolved by the bosses' dark-horse selection of Warren G. Harding—to the utter surprise and eventual consternation of the American people. . . .

The Harding nomination has become the perfect, stock example of convention boss control. Yet, at that very same convention, the delegates refused to accept the choice of the same bosses for the vice presidential candidate, the late Senator Irvine L. Lenroot of Wisconsin. They rebelled openly and excitedly followed a delegate from Oregon, Wallace McCamant, who jumped up on his seat and gave the convention the name of Governor Calvin Coolidge of Massachusetts who became President upon the death of Harding.

This brings up the "how," or mechanics, of securing a nomination for the presidency. The procedure is, in fact, much the same as for any other office, except for the assumed modesty and standoffishness of the usual aspirant for the White House, and it is of course, on a much grander scale.

The first requisite, naturally, is what might be called a "salable" as well as an "available" candidate. Preeminently qualified in this regard are men long prominent in politics and public life, but there are also others—for example, outstanding business men who have won recognition for interest and activity in public affairs, such as a Hoover or Willkie, and even occasionally, as now, a military man of broad gauge such as General Eisenhower.

Then the candidate needs a manager, or a board of managers. These usually are drawn from men with political experience and wide political contacts. They constitute both an advisory board on tactics and strategy and a liaison to deal with state leaders who can assure delegates at the national convention.

The manager or managers also require a publicity staff to tell about the candidate's record, and for all this a headquarters is necessary, usually with branches in various parts of the country. Not the least of the jobs for these managers is to issue statements discounting the significance of temporary setbacks for their candidate or to spread the claim of a popular "ground swell."

This all costs money, and so the managers always include some figure who is adept at raising funds among persons, who, for one reason or another—and sometimes it is the quite unselfish motive of having a part in "making" a President—are willing to invest in what is at best a gamble, even less sure than roulette or horse-racing.

Still, in spite of the best-laid plans, as the convention begins to assemble there are always tense moments when even the most confident aspirants and their managers are wary of the sudden surprise. About the lobbies and corridors of hotels on convention eve, rumors fly of bargains and deals, of doubt of this or that delegation, of last-minute switches. Always, too, there is the attempt of the clever manager to pull off some coup which will create a bandwagon psychology. . . .

Such are the tactics which, up to the convention opening itself, complicate the nominating process, often make mere pawns of delegates, and give the ultimate decision to the influence or personal whim of bosses. The people seem very far away.

The ultimate result varies in its soundness and wisdom. Whereas the dominant influence of bosses gave the Republican party a Warren G. Harding in 1920, the combination of many forces and influences, in which the party rank and file was a factor surely, also gave the Democratic party a Woodrow Wilson and a Franklin D. Roosevelt, and the Republican party a Hoover, a Willkie and a Dewey in recent years.

HOW CONVENTIONS ARE RUN [3]

Q. What is your feeling about all the "hoopla" that goes on at the conventions? Do you think it helps any of the rival candidates?

A. No, I don't. I shall never forget standing in the balcony in 1932 in Chicago when Governor Ritchie was placed in nomination. They put on a great show—a great parade. I walked out on the balcony. He and I stood there alone and I put my arm on his shoulder. I said: "Bert, that's a great reception for you," and just as he saw me he said: "Unfortunately there's not a single delegate in the whole demonstration."

Q. Well, do you think that these conventions will be changed in their external appearance because of television?

A. I think that's true. They listened to radio, starting in 1924. I think that was the first convention where radio was used —to any extent. It will be interesting now to watch the effect of television on the people who are looking at the screens. I don't think it will have any effect on the convention itself. But I'm curious to know what effect it will have on the voting public.

Q. You think it might induce a greater interest on the part of the public in the campaign that follows?

[3] From an interview with James A. Farley, former chairman, Democratic National Committee. *United States News & World Report,* an independent weekly news magazine on national and international affairs published at Washington, D.C. 32:30-6. June 27, 1952. Copyright 1952, United States News Publishing Company. Reprinted by permission.

A. It can't help but produce a greater interest because people can see more through their eyes than they get through their ears. It's bound to have an effect on the election itself. . . .

Q. Do you think that a President in office can bring about his own renomination?

A. I don't think there's any question about it. The President in office always can, if he so desires and he has control of the party. He can bring about his own nomination because I don't think the party would dare reject the candidacy of the President in office if he desires to be named.

Q. You think if it hadn't been for this [twenty-second] constitutional amendment Presidents would have felt free to continue in office as long as they could hold the party machinery together?

A. I don't think there's any doubt about it, because in my talk with Mr. Roosevelt at Hyde Park early in 1940 I told him that in my judgment he could be elected for a third term, a fourth term and, if his health were good, I felt he could run for a fifth term. . . .

Q. Do you think that a candidate could be really drafted nowadays in these party conventions?

A. Well, there you can always say "no." However, there are many people who argue that no man is too big to serve his country, no man is too big to refuse to be nominated for the presidency or the vice presidency. I think that depends in a large measure on the attitude of the individual himself. Is he willing to be drafted or not? You can't be drafted if you definitely say that under no circumstances will you accept the nomination. If you say that definitely before a convention, I don't think that any convention can draft a man. He just does what he likes.

Q. But these drafts depend very largely on the way they are operated, don't they?

A. They depend in a large measure upon the individual himself. Now you and I know that in states they apparently draft a candidate, but with his full knowledge and approval, and set the wheels of the machinery to work, cultivating public opinion along the lines that everybody wants a certain man to make the race for governor or for the Senate.

Q. How much importance do you attribute to the candidate himself getting out in different parts of the country a year or two in advance of the Convention?

A. Sometimes it helps and sometimes it isn't necessary. You remember, Mr. Roosevelt stuck pretty close to his job in Albany. He didn't move around the country very much—not at all before he was nominated—just a few speeches here and there. . . .

Q. Do you think that there exists in this country a large bloc of independent voters who swing from one party to the other in national elections?

A. Yes, I think the elections in a large measure are determined by what might be called a given number of independent voters. You can call them independents. They are party voters, too, if you will. They're in the Democratic and Republican parties and they're pretty sincere partisans. I think there comes a time when they move from one party to the other and I think that that is the group that finally determines who'll be the successful candidate. . . .

Q. Do you share the popular idea that platforms that are written at party conventions are discarded and ignored later on and therefore don't have much significance or importance?

A. I wouldn't go so far as to say that they don't mean anything, but I do really believe that the candidate himself in the campaign means more than the platform. The people have to vote for a man and have faith in his abiltiy to do the job, to carry out the pledge in the party platform to the extent that he is able to do so. Now a set of circumstances may develop and make it impossible for any candidate to carry out the platform completely even though he may be desirous of doing so. The candidate, in my judgment, overshadows the importance of the platform.

Q. Of course, no candidate would veer away from the platform, at least during the campaign, would he?

A. No, he wouldn't. The only case of that kind I can recall was that of Governor Smith, who, after he was nominated in 1928, denounced—he frankly said that he wouldn't take—the platform insofar as it referred to the Eighteenth Amendment.

Q. Turning to the way conventions are run, isn't it true that the delegates, before they come to the convention, are—a good many of them—on the fence as to how they ultimately will vote?

A. As you know, many of the delegates are instructed. Some of the instructions are firm and some not so firm. But in the main I think that most of the delegates before they come to the convention city have their minds pretty well made up which way they would like to vote—in other words, which candidate they would prefer to see nominated.

Q. What is it that switches them during the convention?

A. Well, the fact that their own candidate may get out of the picture because he hasn't a sufficient number of votes to be nominated. Then they gravitate in the direction they want to, and in some cases they have no choice in the matter. The majority come through with another candidate so they go along, not because they want to, but because they feel he's "going to be the nominee anyway." They do like to be on the band-wagon.

Q. Is there much persuading and arguing going on before the balloting starts—trying to get delegations to swing?

A. There isn't any doubt of that. The persuading goes on behind closed doors, in the lobbies and other places.

Q. Well, what do you think is the argument that persuades the delegates when you need a critical delegation to come over to your side?

A. Men go to a convention and they're anxious to nominate the winning candidate, and I think that is the most persuasive argument. They want to see their party win, not only from a national point of view, but from a state point of view, if you will—so that the desire to win, I think, is the dominating factor in the argument. Delegates from different sections of the country get together and find out how the other delegates feel about whether a certain candidate can win. That's about the way it goes.

Q. Does it often happen that in some states there is rivalry between factions in the state, and one might be for one candidate, another for another? How do you work out a situation like that? What technique do you use?

A. You try to get the dominant factions there on your side. You try to get the other factions to go on with the dominating factions, and you assure them that in the event you win they will be treated fairly. You don't make any direct promise. But you try to assure them that we will be fair with everybody who comes along with your side.

There isn't any doubt that after a party comes to power it naturally seems more sympathetic to those who were with you and helped you put over your candidate. Because you feel that they're loyal—you're bound to be considerate to them. By the same token, in my experience, we were not unfair to those who didn't come along.

Q. In these conventions, which last only a few days, is the bulk of the work done before they get to the convention hall or is the major part of your work after the delegates get together and you feel out the various delegations?

A. I think the major part of it is done beforehand. We had a pretty good line on the situation, I think it can truthfully be said, before we went to Chicago in 1932.

Q. Is it considered important for a candidate who has the lead in the race to try to select the temporary chairman and the permanent chairman from among his own supporters?

A. Yes, it's terribly important. I think the temporary chairman in a sense is more important than the permanent chairman. You get the temporary chairman first and the permanent chairman, of course, afterwards.

In the many motions that have to be made, the chairman can see over the head of the fellow he doesn't want to recognize to the fellow he wants to put the motions. That's done in legislative halls, as you know, and more or less accepted by those in the conventions. In other words, it's like the Speaker in the House. He recognizes the persons he feels should be recognized, whom he may have advised on the subject. That's true of conventions in both parties. The fellow who loses out, of course, doesn't like it, but he knows full well that, if he were at the pole with the majority, he would do the same thing under like circumstances.

Q. Do you think there is any advantage in the so-called keynote speeches when your own man is selected as temporary chairman and as permanent chairman?

A. I think the speeches are not as important as the fact that you have a temporary or permanent chairman who is sympathetic to your cause and your candidate. The speeches might have effect so far as the individual speaker is concerned, but, as for effect on the result of the convention—I think not.

Q. Would you say it is important to have control of a majority of the Resolutions Committee that frames the platform?

A. Oh, I think that's very important.

Q. Why is that?

A. Well, because, in the first place, you want to try to have a committee write a platform that will more or less be tied in with the candidate you are trying to nominate. If you had a good many resolutions in the platform that would make it difficult for your nominee to stand on, you'd be in lots of trouble.

Q. Is it because the platform is adopted before the roll call on the candidates and it might be more in keeping with the views of a particular candidate and he might get an advantage? Is that it?

A. Yes, it's bound to be that way. So it's highly important that you try to have a platform that your particular candidate will be able to stand on and not be embarrassed.

Q. Is that the reason why the minority reports are brought in to the Platform Committee so as to make it possible for the convention to select some other candidate than the dominant one?

A. That's always the case.

Q. Speaking of conventions in general, isn't it a risky thing for your side, and a dangerous thing, if some of your own supporters, all in one delegation, one state, start slipping away from you?

A. There isn't any doubt that that has a psychological effect, because I remember very distinctly on the first ballot in 1932, when we nominated Roosevelt, we didn't give all our votes. We had votes in Missouri and some other places, and we made a gain on the second ballot, if you look over the roll call, and then again on the third ballot. Slight though the gain was, we made a gain on each ballot because we wanted to show that we had strength in the convention coming to us on each ballot and we did that definitely for a psychological reason.

Q. The public sometimes thinks you are gaining spontaneously when actually it's part of your preconceived strategy?

A. Yes, that's right. The public doesn't understand that, and some of your own people don't understand that. As a matter of fact you can't tell everybody around you what the story is because, after two or three people have a secret—you know what it is with secrets! As a matter of fact, there were very few people opposed to us in the convention who knew we were talking with the Garner group. Actually we talked with the Garner people before we started to ballot. We were hoping very much we could get them to come along on the first ballot.

Q. They knew they couldn't nominate Garner for President; they didn't have enough votes for that?

A. That's right; and Garner, of course, knew that and he didn't want a repetition of what happened in 1924 in the New York convention.

Q. Do you think that the techniques and the tactics are any different in the Republican conventions than the Democratic?

A. No, I think they're the same. They have to be the same— the same rules apply, the same conditions apply, it's the same situation. They do it the same as we do; they play with different characters, but it's the same system.

Q. And do you think that this matter of persuading delegations to come over to you is the real job that has to be done at conventions?

A. That's the real job. It's the real job of the campaign manager and those who are working with him.

Q. What tools or ammunition does he really have at his disposal in order to bring that about? What has he got to offer these various delegations that may not have a vice-presidential candidate?

A. Well, he tries to sell them the idea that it is better for their party to go along with his particular candidate because it would help strengthen their organization, maybe help to elect the governor, maybe help them elect congressmen, or a senator, or any other legislative offices. The leader of the party is the leader of the campaign, and the campaign manager of the nominee does everything he possibly can to assure that the organization is in good order because, after they nominate the candidate, they must elect him.

Q. How far do you think that we would get if we had a system of nation-wide presidential-preference primaries so that the delegates were all chosen by some primary system?

A. There are a lot of arguments for the preferential primary of that type and a lot of arguments on both sides, but I haven't thought about it sufficiently to give a considered answer.

Q. Well, what is your experience with states where they do have primaries? Do the delegates stand hitched?

A. They do where the law compels them to—in some places such as California they have to stand hitched, until such time as the nominee selected in the primary releases them. As in the case of Senator McAdoo in 1932—he had to release the delegates to Mr. Roosevelt. Now, in some of the states, as you know, it is more of a popularity contest, so to speak. I don't think that the delegates are bound. I won the delegation of Massachusetts in the 1940 primary, but ten or fifteen or twenty of these delegates, under pressure, voted for Mr. Roosevelt.

Q. When you look over the personnel of the delegations and the various conventions with which you had experience, would you say that they are composed for the most part of people active in politics?

A. I would say that 95 per cent of the men [and women] who go there—many of them go there as delegates—are men and women who are actively engaged in politics either as office-holders or contributors. Most of the men who go there on the Democratic side are men who are recognized for their services to the party in some form or other.

Q. And do these state delegations have frequent meetings during the convention?

A. Well, at the start of the convention, before the convention gets under way, there's a rule that the delegation meets and they have a sort of caucus to determine who will represent their state on such committees as the Resolutions Committee and the Committee on Permanent Organization and the Credentials Committee.

Q. Is it important that some of the people in these delegations get to second nominations and to make brief speeches in order to get recognition back home?

A. Well, they try to do that. They try to see that those men and women who back home are rather strong and active in the party get recognition sometimes. Some are particularly qualified to make good speeches. But they try to recognize men in the convention who are entitled to recognition in relation to their services in the party.

Q. Would you say the national convention differs very much from the state and county conventions?

A. No, they're exactly alike.

Q. Are the tactics and procedures somewhat similar?

A. I think they're exactly the same.

Q. How far do you think—how successful do you think this convention system has been in nominating the man that the party really wanted? In most instances is that done or are there compromises that don't represent the true will?

A. I don't think in every case it has been done but I think, in the main, the delegates have done honestly what they thought was for the best interest of the party. That's been so in both parties. They get bitterness such as the 1924 Democratic convention deadlock, which led to the nomination of John W. Davis, or in 1912, when Mr. Wilson was nominated. In 1940, if Senator Taft and Governor Dewey could have decided which would run for President and which for Vice President, then Wendell Willkie wouldn't have had his chance.

Q. Do you think, in your experience, that the vice-presidential nomination is given the consideration that it deserves?

A. I don't think that in every convention it is. In 1932, in my judgment, the nominee was the most qualified man for Vice President. Mr. Garner had a long and successful career in public life.

Q. Why didn't he go along to become the Vice President for the third term?

A. He [Mr. Garner] felt exactly as I did against a third term.

Q. You've been vindicated, haven't you, by the adoption of a constitutional amendment limiting presidential terms to two?

A. Well, I'm not so pleased so far as being vindicated is concerned, but I have very deep-seated ideas on the subject. I was gratified that the people of this country, acting through their state legislatures, adopted the limiting amendment.

Q. What is your opinion about the accuracy of sampling political opinion by various polls?

A. I consider that, in the main, the polls are accurate and are certainly intended to be accurate by those who conduct them. Now it may be possible the human element enters into it as it does in everything else, and maybe some of those employed taking the poll may get careless here and there. There's certainly no favoritism desired on the part of those who take the poll and I do think that they honestly make an effort to get the opinion of the vote.

Q. In other words, they want to be right?

A. They must be right because if they're not right it's a reflection on the newspaper or whatever group takes the polls. And in future polls the public would have no respect for their opinion.

Q. Do you think that the scientific type of poll, such as that of George Gallup, of taking a small sampling of the electorate, is the right approach?

A. Well, as far as I know, it's the only approach. And I think I may repeat that they've done pretty well. Of course, to the successful candidate it's good news, but to the fellow who's losing it isn't good. Now there are a lot of people who argued that these polls have an effect on the voters, and I'm inclined to think that possibly they do because there are any number of people who like to be on the winning side, and if they feel their party is going to win they are more likely to go along than if they feel they're going to lose.

Q. You think that when these polls come out, as they some-times do, in the last few days of a campaign they stimulate one party or the other to greater effort?

A. Yes, I think it helps the party that looks as if it's going to win, and, as for the party it shows is going to lose, I do think it has an effect on the workers within the party—in other words, the committee workers, the precinct workers. If it shows a close fight, they'll work harder for their candidate to get their votes to the polls, but, if it shows that the candidate is in a lot of diffi-culty, they may not exert the last effort to get the last vote in the precinct or the district to the polling place.

In other words, if in a district there are ten voters who haven't voted and it looks as if it is a close vote, the worker will try to get those ten. If the poll shows that his party is in a bad way, he'll proceed to tell you, "Well, I did the best I could. If they don't want him, well, I won't make the last effort." It could have an effect. In the state of New York above the Bronx line, you could have many thousands of election districts where three or four votes in an election district affects the winner or loser in the state.

WHAT CONVENTIONS SHOULD DO [4]

Our convention method of choosing candidates and drawing up platforms has many advantages over the caucus method. It is more democratic. It serves to dramatize and advertise the issues and leaders. It focuses the interest of the country on particular men and questions. And the convention usually manages to com-promise dangerous issues within a party rather than inject them into the national arena.

Let us look at the history of some of the more dramatic of our conventions for illustrations of these things. In 1860 the Republican party was new, and it had a good chance of victory. The important thing was to select a candidate who would win

[4] From "When Parties Stand or Fall," by Henry Steele Commager, professor of history, Columbia University. *Senior Scholastic.* 53:17. October 13, 1948. Reprinted from Scholastic Magazines by permission of the editors.

moderate as well as extreme antislavery support and who would not frighten the South out of the Union.

The most prominent of the candidates was Governor William H. Seward of New York, long the leading figure in the new party. After him came men like Salmon P. Chase of Ohio, and Abraham Lincoln of Illinois. The Lincoln supporters, though not perhaps the most numerous, were the most devoted, the best organized, and the noisiest.

Lincoln came from the Middle West, the center of Republican strength. He seemed to be a moderate, not an extremist on slavery as Seward and Chase were supposed to be. Because he was less known, he had few enemies. His humble birth, his democratic simplicity, his homely wit, all made him a good candidate. To the surprise of Easterners, he won on the third ballot.

This convention dramatized the new party and brought Lincoln prominently before the country. It fought out, within itself, the antislavery issue that might have divided it.

The Democratic convention of the same year was a real knock-down, drag-out fight, in which the extremists won. The majority supported Stephen A. Douglas of Illinois—an experienced and moderate statesman who wanted to avoid the slavery issue and concentrate on other things. But a fanatical minority refused to go along with the Douglas majority, bolted the convention, held its own convention, and nominated an extremist, John Breckenridge. The Douglas Democrats adjourned from Charleston, South Carolina, to Baltimore, where they nominated Douglas. So there were two Democratic parties in the field. This meant Republican victory.

Here was a convention which did not compromise its differences within the party, but broke up and took them before the country. It did not allow the majority to have its way. The result was disaster.

Another crucial convention year was 1912. Then there was widespread discontent with the power of great corporations and with the alleged failure of the government to control railroads and trusts. President William H. Taft was in the White House

—a staunch, though open-minded, conservative who had allied the Republican party with big business.

Theodore Roosevelt, who had put Taft into the presidency in 1908, was now determined to get him out. In 1911 he decided to make the race himself. He entered the primaries in thirteen states, and wherever he ran, he proved more popular than Taft.

Yet when the convention came around it was clear that it was in the hands of the Old Guard. Blind to the upsurge of progressivism in the nation they threw out many of T.R.'s delegates and proceeded to "steam-roller" Taft into the nomination. T.R. determined to bolt the party and run on his own ticket.

The Progressive (Bull Moose) party convention met in the atmosphere of a camp meeting. "We stand at Armageddon and we battle for the Lord," shouted Roosevelt. Roosevelt was nominated by acclamation, and began his fight for an independent liberal party.

The failure of the Republicans to settle their differences within the party meant a split that made a Democratic victory almost certain. The two most prominent Democratic candidates were Champ Clark of Missouri, an old-line regular and conservative, and Woodrow Wilson of New Jersey, new to politics but pretty clearly progressive in his point of view.

From the beginning, the Democratic convention was dominated by William Jennings Bryan. He had been three times a candidate, and three times defeated. Yet so great was his hold over his followers that he was still the outstanding figure in the party. He was determined that, now the Promised Land was in sight, it should be entered under the leadership of a progressive. Before the convention met he had sent telegrams to all candidates asking them to pledge themselves to a progressive program. Only Wilson's answer satisfied Bryan.

Bryan came from Nebraska, and the Nebraska delegates were pledged to Clark. Wilson and Clark were neck and neck at the start, with Clark slightly in the lead. On the tenth ballot New York swung her powerful delegation to Clark, and for the first time he had a clear majority. But the Democratic party required a two-thirds vote for the nomination.

On the thirteenth ballot Bryan ascended the platform to "explain" his vote. He announced to a thunderstruck convention that, since the reactionaries were supporting Clark, he was throwing his support to Wilson. Pandemonium broke forth, and Wilson began to gain strength. Finally on the forty-sixth ballot Wilson was nominated.

The Democratic convention had succeeded, where the Republican had failed, in compromising its issues within the party itself. The result was, of course, the triumphant election of Wilson at the polls that fall.

The moral of the stories of 1860 and 1912 is clear enough. Parties, and conventions, should be democratic institutions in which the majority has its way, in which issues are clarified and compromised, and through which strong candidates can be decided upon.

A PRACTICAL POLITICAL DEVICE [5]

The national party conventions are, I believe, a vital part of the American political system. Smoke-filled rooms are indispensable to their successful operation. The convention must be improved, not weakened. We must make more use of it, not less. . . .

Those who look aghast at convention horse-trades and hijinks often forget that compromise is the very essence of democratic politics. Some of the deals may not be pretty ones, but in any case bargaining and even manipulation are inevitable. The convention is simply the arena where the final negotiations take place, subject to a number of ground rules. . . .

The smoke-filled room is essential to the convention for it serves as the mechanism that allows party leaders to shift their choices toward a compromise candidate. Without such a mechanism there would be eternal deadlock. The Democratic convention of 1924, which went through 103 harrowing roll-calls

[5] From "The Case for the Smoke-Filled Room," by James MacGregor Burns, chairman of the political science department, Williams College. New York *Times Magazine*. p9+. June 15, 1952. Reprinted by permission.

before settling on a candidate, might have done its job better with more smoke-filled rooms, not fewer.

Is there any way to achieve party compromise and unity without all this bargaining and maneuvering? The only real alternative to the convention system is a nation-wide direct presidential primary system. President Woodrow Wilson in 1913 advocated legislation providing for primary elections throughout the country "at which the voters of the several parties may choose their nominees for the presidency without the intervention of nominating conventions." Similar proposals have been made more recently.

The difficulties with such a plan are twofold. It would not guarantee an end to "boss control"; experience with primaries has proved that party organizations often can dominate primary elections as easily as they dominate conventions. More important, primary elections on a national scale could disrupt party solidarity and effectiveness. They might allow organized groups to move in and take over control of party selections. Candidates of such groups are often poorly equipped to lead a united party in the general election or to command firm party backing in office.

The point is that we need consensus *within* the party so that all major elements—geographical, economic, ideological—can take part in choosing party leaders and shaping party goals. We need division between the major parties so that the people will have a meaningful choice at the polls. The primary system often gives us the reverse. It disrupts party consensus by foisting on the party candidates who may be alien to party traditions and principles. It may produce candidates in the fall elections who are either so close to each other in viewpoint that the voters see little choice between them, or so far apart that the voters look in desperation for some middle ground.

Primaries, moreover, cannot perform an important job that the convention can—the adoption of a party platform. It is fashionable to deride the platform as a useless collection of platitudes, resembling a train platform in that it is "something to get in on, not to stand on." If this were the case, hard-headed politicians would not sweat over the planks as hard as they do. Actually the platforms are important because they tell, in Herbert Agar's words, "not what a party will do, but who is pushing and pulling for what, and with how much success."

Does all this mean that we should give the convention a clean bill of health? Not at all. Political scientists and practical politicians alike have urged the following improvements:

(1) Make the conventions more representative. Too many delegates are allowed from states where the parties have little strength. Both parties give a "bonus" to areas where they are strong but apportionment of delegates still is far from perfect.

(2) Make the conventions smaller. Around 3,000 delegates and alternate delegates . . . [crowded] into each of the major conventions . . . [in 1952]. One third of this number would allow for more orderly and coherent deliberation. Party conventions should never become small, however, because one of their chief functions is to whip up enthusiasm that will send the party workers home eager for the battle to come.

(3) Make more use of the convention. The greatest weakness of the convention is that it meets only once every four years. This seems a bit ridiculous when one considers that small business, labor and professional organizations assemble at least annually. The convention should meet every year in order to invigorate the party organization and to bring the platform up to date. The minority party should use the occasion to nominate a leader to organize opposition to the party in power. Nothing would improve our convention system more than fuller use of it.

So much for needed reforms in the convention itself. At least as desirable are changes in the methods of selecting delegates to conventions. This phase of the convention system has aroused the most criticism. The indictment is twofold: first, that methods of choosing delegates are baffling to the voters and discourage them from taking part; second, that the bosses actually choose and control delegates and the people are left out.

The first charge is true. The average voter in a presidential primary finds a ballot covered with names of people he does not know and whose positions on either candidates or principles are not clear. Delegates to be elected are in all stages of commitment to some candidate, of semicommitment, or of no commitment at all. . . . The whole system of electing delegates needs to be enormously simplified. Moreover, eligibility requirements for voters should be clarified to prevent fracases and misunderstandings such as the recent ones between Taft and Eisenhower supporters in the South.

The second charge bears close examination. Certainly one can find a good deal of "boss control" in the selection of delegates, but as in most of our political processes, there is a good deal of both democracy and oligarchy in the system, and it is hard to tell where one ends and the other begins.

Methods of electing delegates fall broadly into two types. About one third of the states have presidential preference primaries. These primaries give the voters some chance to indicate their choice among candidates, as in the case of the . . . primaries in New Hampshire and South Dakota. In the other states, delegates are chosen in party conventions or committees.

We are told that the first system is fair and democratic and that the second system is boss-controlled and undemocratic. Is this true? Some of the presidential primaries are rigged and run by a handful of professionals. The choices are so arranged and the ballot is so set up that the election results often misrepresent the voters' real views. Such primaries thoroughly deserved to be described by President Truman's term "eyewash." Some state convention procedures, on the other hand, are democratic and aboveboard. They produce delegations that fairly represent the views of the party rank and file.

The hub of the matter is this: both the primary system and the state convention system *can* be democratic methods. Both *can* become "boss-controlled." Whether they become one or the other depends on whether and how the voters use them. Those who complain about bossism are usually the same ones who, a few months back, were sitting by idly while others did the party chores. The most democratic appearing gadgets in the world will not do the job if they lack the propulsive power of wide participation by the people.

Whatever method is used, it should not unduly limit the delegates' freedom of action. Those rules that bind delegates to a certain candidate "until hell freezes over" defeat the whole purpose of the national convention. There must be room for maneuver. . . .

The national party convention in its present form is well over a century old. A peculiarly American institution, it has had many triumphs and a few failures. Like most of the devices of democracy, the system works about as well as the people make it work.

WHERE COMPROMISES ARE MADE [6]

Appeasement, conciliation, compromise—whichever word you prefer, the thing itself is the essence of politics in a democratic government. In many countries, such as France for example, the compromises are between the various groups or parties, and are negotiated in the legislative bodies as part of the process of legislation. So they are in the United States also. But in the United States the fundamental compromises are in the first instance made not between the major parties but within them; and the place where these initial compromises are made is in the national nominating conventions.

The national nominating convention is something unknown to the Constitution and undreamed of by the Founding Fathers. It is an American invention, as native to the United States of America as corn pone or apple pie. A Democratic or a Republican national nominating convention, once it gets going, emits sounds and lights that never were on land or sea. Superficially observed, it has all the variety of a slithy tove. At different hours of the day or night it has something of the painted and tinseled and tired gaiety of a four-ring circus, something of the juvenile inebriety and synthetic fraternal sentiment of a class reunion, something of the tub-thumping emotional frenzy of a backwoods camp meeting. For patriotic oratory unrestrained, for indulgence

[6] From "The Will of the People," by Carl Becker, late professor emeritus of history, Cornell University. *Yale Review*. 34, no3:385-404. Spring [March] 1945. Reprinted by permission.

in exaggerated compliment or vituperation as brazen as it is dis-
ingenuous, for general blare and blarney and pandemonium, a national nominating convention has, as a college student bursting
with admiration and bad grammar once said of a favorite professor, "few equals and no peers."

But all this is on the surface and in the public eye. What
goes on beneath the surface and behind locked doors is something both realistic and important. For it is here, unexposed to
the public eye, that the deals and bargains, the necessary compromises are arranged—compromises designed to satisfy as well
as possible all divergent elements within the party. In both
major parties the compromises are essentially the same, since they
are between the same divergent elements—conservatives and progressives, agriculture and industry, capital and labor, East, South,
Middle West, and Far West. And since these divergent elements
within each party correspond to the divergent interests within
the nation, what really goes on in a national nominating convention is the attempt, by the party leaders, to forecast the intangible
and uncertain will of the people, as it will be registered in state
pluralities, and to shape the party policies in conformity with it.

The visible results of this effort are two—the candidate and
the platform. Often enough the platform is an object of derision
and the candidate a figure of fun. But they are what the compromises and the forecast call for—the best available bids for
votes where votes are at a premium. It is, of course, desirable
that the candidate finally chosen should be a distinguished statesman who would rather be right than be president, but it is a
curious and significant fact that more distinguished statesmen of
the right sort have been found in New York, Illinois, Ohio and
Indiana than anywhere else, and none at all, since the Civil War
at least, in the solid South. The platform is often, one might say
always, derided because it fails to formulate a clear-cut concrete
program based upon discernible principles. This is, however, to
mistake the purpose of a platform altogether. The purpose of
a platform is not to formulate a program of action but to find
out what program, if any, the people by and large will be disposed to support. A platform . . . is a formula setting forth the

position of the party on the political controversies of the moment
—a formula which must be sufficiently general to be acceptable
to all shades of opinion, and sufficiently ambiguous to permit all
and sundry to cling to their private heresies and still to be
counted among the faithful. The purpose of a platform is to
win as many votes as possible, and still leave the party, in case
it wins the election, free to adopt whatever concrete measures the
changed conditions seem to demand and the prevailing sentiment
of the country will support.

The function of a major political party is thus to fathom and
represent as well as may be that intangible and illusive thing
called "the will of the people." Both of the present major parties
perform that function with remarkable success; and either party
can lead the nation because—to paraphrase a famous saying of
Edmund Burke—its existence depends on knowing with a high
degree of accuracy in what direction and how rapidly the nation
is willing to go. In this sense, the two major parties between
them represent the will of the people; and since there is no
fundamental difference between them, either in principles pro-
fessed or policies advocated, one of them represents it about as
well as the other; if one party rather than the other wins a particular national election, it is only by virtue of being, in July, a
little more expert in guessing what "general directive" the voters,
registering their will by concurrent pluralities in the states, will
issue on the first Tuesday after the first Monday in the following
November.

It is partly for this reason that the result of a presidential
election, whichever party wins, is as far as possible from being
a revolution. Both parties have appealed to all classes and all
pressure groups for support; both have made essentially similar
compromises in order to win such support; and as a consequence
both have of necessity taken their stand on platforms that differ
very little, except in the fact that one defends the record of the
party in power while the other attacks it, or maybe in the fact
that one, in its phraseology, exhibits an ambiguity less subtle and
more open to derision than the other.

PLEA FOR A NATIONAL PRIMARY [7]

I believe the proposal for a national presidential primary has a greater chance for success if we advance it first as a general principle, then work out the details after the reform has been approved by constitutional referendum. For this reason, I purposely kept my resolution simple and nonspecific as to details. I have in mind, however, a pattern for a nation-wide presidential primary, and I will work for adoption of a bill along such lines if the basic idea is adopted as a constitutional amendment.

My plan is as follows:

Step One: There shall be a primary in every state, provided for by Federal law, to determine the popular choice of the people for President. In each primary, delegates shall be elected to cast their votes at a streamlined national convention for the choice of their state's voters.

Discussion: There have been presidential primaries in various states since Wisconsin passed the first such state law in 1903. Currently, nineteen states have primary laws of one sort or another. The laws, however, are not uniform, and in some states are not even binding on the delegates; the lack of uniformity, plus the fact that most of the states do not have primaries, leads to a helter-skelter pattern that prompted Mr. Truman, just before the New Hampshire primary, to brand presidential primaries as "eyewash."

With a uniform and binding law applicable to every state, presidential primaries no longer would be "eyewash," but would be meaningful. Mr. Truman, incidentally, has endorsed the principle of national primaries, as did the late Woodrow Wilson.

Step Two: No candidate shall be placed on the ballot in any state primary without his consent, and he must file a qualifying petition signed by not less than one per cent of the total number of voters who voted for the presidential candidate of his party in the last election.

[7] From "Why Not Let the People Elect Our President?", by Senator Estes Kefauver, (Democrat, Tennessee), and Sidney Shalett, free-lance writer on Washington affairs. *Collier's*. 131:34-9. January 31, 1953. Reprinted by permission.

Discussion: This provision would make it necessary for a man to be a willing candidate and to work for his nomination. I believe it is a good principle, and a democratic one, for "the man to seek the job"—particularly under the proposed new system where the voters really would have something to say about selection of candidates. It also will eliminate many of the nonserious candidates—"favorite sons" and others.

Step Three: A uniform nation-wide system of choosing delegates, based on the vote of the political party of each state in the previous presidential election, shall be adopted. There shall be provisions to limit the number of delegates so as to avoid the present unwieldy size of national conventions, and there shall be no split votes—such as one-half and one-third votes.

Discussion: It would be politically healthy to peg a state's delegates to the total votes mustered by the party in the last election. For one thing, the system would strike a blow at local bosses, who sometimes actually connive to keep down the total vote, because of the greater dictatorship they can exercise when only a few citizens vote.

I suggest that, instead of the present 1,200-odd votes at a convention, with some of them split between two and three delegates, the total be limited to no more than 600, with no split votes. It is impossible to conduct an orderly convention with some 2,000 (counting the split votes) delegates—not to mention their alternates—milling about.

Step Four: Delegates shall be firmly pledged to cast their votes on a proportional basis geared to the state vote received by the candidate. As a simple illustration, if a state has ten delegates and Candidate A receives approximately 60 per cent of the vote, he will receive six votes at a convention. (To avoid undesirable fractional ballots, machinery can be set up whereby the division of delegates is calculated by round numbers, rather than by exact fractions.) The delegates will continue to vote for the candidate to whom they are pledged as long as he receives as many as 10 per cent of the total vote cast at the convention (with certain provisions in case of deadlock).

Discussion: I gave thought to the alternate possibility of having the candidate who receives a plurality of the state vote capture all the state delegates. I believe, however, that proportional division is fairer, and would reflect the wishes of the voters more accurately. Such a division is more in line with the belief of many legislators, myself included, that the electoral college vote should be divided proportionately, rather than letting the candidate who gets the most popular votes in a state take all of the state's electoral votes.

Another possible alternative, which might be considered as an interim measure pending reform of the electoral college machinery, would be a Federal primary law patterned after the excellent Wisconsin state law. In Wisconsin, the candidate receiving the largest state-wide vote wins a certain number of delegates running as the state delegates at large, while winners in various congressional districts get the votes of delegates for those districts.

As a means of breaking an early deadlock, a candidate should be given discretionary authority to release his delegates when he feels he cannot win. The law should be written to indicate strongly that the delegates, once released, are free agents, at liberty to exercise their best judgment as to preference among the remaining eligible candidates; the practice of trading delegates to accomplish private political deals should be discouraged.

Step Five: Nomination for President shall be by a simple majority of the total number of votes cast by delegates at the convention. If no candidate has a majority, and has not released his delegates, after ten ballots the delegates shall be considered free of their obligation to vote for the winner of their state primary, but must vote for one of the candidates receiving the top three total number of votes in the national primary.

Discussion: This step provides a key which makes the proposed system practical. In combination with Step Four, it would mitigate the "nuisance value" of any surviving favorite sons, who could not hope to hang on for ten ballots, but would try to trade delegates for favors. The provision for picking the presidential nominee from the aspirants who placed first, second and third in the nation-wide primary popular vote is a means of respecting the will of the voters. It also has constitutional precedent, for the Twelfth Amendment provides that, in the case of a deadlock in the electoral college, the House of Representatives shall elect a president from among the top three candidates.

Step Six: Finally, after the presidential nominee is chosen, the vice-presidential nominee shall be chosen by a vote of the delegates from the three candidates who polled the next highest number of votes in the nation-wide primaries.

Discussion: This proposal is made in an effort to respect the wishes of the electorate; if adopted, it would keep nonentities out of the vice-presidential office, and effectively curb the practice of degrading the office of Vice President to an object of political barter. It would mean that the vice-presidential post would go to a man sufficiently interested in public service to get out and work for his nomination in a primary, and that the post would be filled by a man whom the people knew, and who was of sufficient stature to have placed at least fourth in the national presidential primary. . . .

One of my colleagues, Senator George Smathers of Florida, who also has introduced a bill favoring presidential primaries, has proposed that, if a Vice President succeeds to the presidency by reason of death, there shall be a special presidential election at the next general election to choose a new President. This procedure, in my opinion, would be cumbersome. The system by which one of the top four choices of the victorious party would become Vice President would eliminate the necessity for such a special election.

Another healthy reform that could evolve naturally from such a program would be a shorter campaign period for the men finally chosen by the major parties as presidential nominees. The party candidates would fight it out in the primaries, which would be held simultaneously throughout the country on a fixed date in August. The national conventions then could be held in September. Assuming that the successful candidates would take the usual amount of time to map out their campaign, the actual campaigning could be limited pretty much to the month of October. That plan would be good life insurance for our chief executive.

Personally, I would like to see all campaigning elevated to a less strenuous, more intellectual level, with less wear and tear on the candidates.

I have never seen any sense in practically killing off our presidents before we elect them, and I do not believe the American people really want that. . . .

Critics may argue that the strain of running in forty-eight separate primaries might kill a candidate. I do not think so, particularly with the advent of television. The campaign in each state need not be as intense as the full-dress presidential campaign. And, when the successful candidates of the major parties finally enter upon the shorter campaign to decide the election, both they and what they stood for would be so well known to the voters that the campaign actually would be easier. It could be conducted on a higher plane, involving issues rather than personalities.

Others may contend that, with a national primary system, the race might go to the candidate with the biggest organization and the most money. Again, I disagree. Certainly with scant organization and very little money, I fared well in the primaries I entered. How well that was demonstrated in Nebraska! There, my opponent, Senator Kerr, was able to blanket me with campaign literature, professional workers, entertainment, newspaper advertisements, radio and TV time. In Omaha, I remember, the opposition even bought up all the advertising space on the sides of the city trash cans. Yet, even with the trash cans against me, I captured more than 60 per cent of the votes.

WHAT PRIMARIES SHOULD DO [8]

The principal current use of the presidential primary—to test the relative strength of candidates for nomination—was not the major purpose for which it was designed. The original purpose was to give the voters a direct voice, and ultimately the dominant voice, in selection of nominees for the highest elective office, instead of leaving the choice to "party bosses in smoke-filled rooms" at national conventions. Thus the presidential primary had a common basis with direct election of United States senators, recall of public officials by popular vote, and the initiative and

[8] From "Presidential Primaries," by Roma K. McNickle, staff researcher, *Editorial Research Reports*. *Editorial Research Reports*. 1, no3:49-59. Washington, D.C., January 16, 1952. Reprinted by permission.

referendum, all of which developed during the early years of the
century as part of the progressive movement for popular control
of government in the United States. . . .

Many state presidential primary laws have been amended and
reamended since their first adoption. Some were passed to meet
special local situations. As a result, no two laws are identical.
However, the present laws may be grouped according to whether
presidential primaries are used solely to elect delegates to conventions, or to allow direct popular choice among candidates for
nomination, or both.

I. Primaries devoted solely to electing delegates to national
conventions: (A) Pledged delegates: California, Minnesota (district delegates only), Ohio, Wisconsin. (B) Unpledged delegates: New York (district delegates only). (C) Pledged or unpledged delegates: Florida, Massachusetts (district delegates
only), New Jersey, South Dakota.

II. Primaries with presidential preference vote and election
of delegates to national conventions: (A) Delegates bound by
preference vote: Nebraska, Oregon. (B) Delegates unpledged:
Illinois (district only), Pennsylvania, West Virginia. (C) Delegates pledged or unpledged: New Hampshire.

III. Primary with preference vote and election of delegates
to state conventions: Maryland.

All of these primaries are mandatory for both parties except
in Florida. In the states with optional primaries, Alabama voters
elect pledged or unpledged delegates. Georgia and Arkansas
voters can, at the option of state committees, register a choice
between candidates for the presidential nominations.

The record of presidential primaries as indicators of the
subsequent choice of candidates by the party conventions has
fallen far below original expectations. For the ten presidential
campaigns since 1912, when primary states first elected a significant number of delegates, Republican conventions have
selected a nominee other than the victor in the primaries at least
half the time. . . .

In conventions of the Democratic party the record is somewhat clouded by operation of the two-thirds rule which governed
their choice of candidates through 1936. Woodrow Wilson

polled more votes in the 1912 primaries than Champ Clark, but won the nomination only on the forty-sixth ballot. Former Secretary of the Treasury McAdoo ran far ahead of other candidates in the 1924 primaries but was not able to win a two-thirds majority of the delegates. The 1924 nomination finally went to John W. Davis, who had not been entered in any primary.

Reasons why presidential primaries often fail to lay an unavoidable mandate upon the national conventions are not far to seek. Only one fourth of the states require that presidential primaries be held. While the psychological effect of these primaries on the choice of delegates in other states and on the actions of delegates at the conventions appears undeniable in many campaigns, the proportion of the delegates sent to the conventions by primary states is too small to be decisive unless almost all are supporting the same candidate.

Furthermore, not all the primary states afford the opportunity to choose among all leading contenders for the nominations. Primaries run from early March (filing closes in January in two states) until a few weeks before the summer conventions. Some aspirants prefer to keep their hats out of the ring until at least the first few primaries have been held.

Many candidates, out of courtesy or prudence, refrain from entering the primary of a state with a strong "favorite son." Stassen made enemies among Republican leaders by entering the Ohio primary in 1948 when Taft was running. His victory over MacArthur in Wisconsin might have been less decisive had the general been at hand to campaign in the state which claims him as its own.

It has been deemed politically inadvisable to enter actively into a contest for delegates in states where other candidates have great popularity, even though they are not favorite sons. In such cases it seems wiser to negotiate with state leaders for second-choice support in later ballots at the conventions, when first-ballot favorites may have fallen by the wayside. Obviously the results of a primary where voters have no chance to express themselves on leading candidates, except through write-in votes, may not measure correctly sentiment within the state itself, let alone throw light on probable action of conventions.

These weaknesses of the presidential primary system as it now operates are due to its limited application and to political realities. Perhaps more important is the inability of the voters in the primaries to control actions of the delegates they elect. In only six states must delegates be pledged to vote for a specific candidate. Laws of four states require that elected delegates be unpledged. In all other primary states, delegates may be either pledged or unpledged.

Nor does the preference vote for choice among candidates always serve to control the subsequent actions of delegates as it does under the laws of Nebraska and Oregon. Illinois Republicans in 1948 gave 324,000 votes to R. A. Bender, a political unknown; 6,700 to MacArthur; 1,600 to Stassen; 1,000 to Dewey; 700 to Taft. All of the state's 56 unpledged delegates voted for Governor Green on the first ballot at Philadelphia; on the second ballot 50 of them switched to Taft and 5 to Dewey. . . .

Election of delegates and preferential voting by congressional districts also works to confuse the picture. The classic example is the election by an Illinois district in 1920 of an avowed supporter of Senator Johnson (Republican, California) as its delegate to the convention, while General Leonard Wood was winning the district's presidential preference vote, and Governor Frank Lowden was winning the preference vote of the state as a whole.

It should be noted also that, while voters in all states elect directly those delegates who represent congressional districts, delegates at large are chosen by the party organizations in Illinois, Massachusetts, Minnesota and New York. In many states all the alternate delegates are so chosen. Hence if the state machine does not favor the candidate who wins the state's preference vote or the largest number of district delegates, it is in a position to send to the convention delegates of contrary opinion who can bring pressure on the elected delegates.

Another feature which may tend to weaken the presidential primary as a method of popular control over nominations is the variation of provisions in state laws with regard to consent of candidates whose names (or those of their pledged delegates) appear on the ballot. While most state laws require specific consent by candidates, names may appear without their consent in Illinois and Oregon if enough voters sign petitions on their behalf. Consent is not required in Pennsylvania. In New Hampshire, a candidate whose supporters file a petition must withdraw within ten days of notification if his name is not to appear. Thus in these states, most of which have primaries early in the year, voters may indicate preference for a man who is definitely not a candidate or has not yet made up his mind to run. On the other hand, it can be argued that these state laws further popular control of nominations by allowing voters to "draft" candidates of their choice. (Several states provide space on the presidential primary ballot for write-in votes.)

Despite its weaknesses, many political economists believe the presidential primary has useful features which should commend it to non-primary states. Some of the advantages were well demonstrated in the Nebraska "people's primary" of 1948, which brought all the leading candidates into the state, giving the voters a chance to hear, see and question them. . . . Possibly because the delegates had informally pledged themselves to follow the preference vote and citizens therefore knew that their choice would have meaning, they turned out in record numbers, casting 185,000 votes as compared with the previous all-time high of 65,000 in 1940.

If more states had the Nebraska type of campaign, it is held that local opinion on national issues, as shown in the primary vote, could give the conventions valuable assistance in drafting the platforms and generally determining party policy. This contribution would be an addition to the present practical opportunities for the parties to see how candidates register with the public outside their own states.

Merriam and Gosnell [Charles E. Merriam and Harold F. Gosnell, *The American Party System,* 1949] believe that a first step in strengthening the presidential primary system might be to hold all primaries at or very near the same time. The theory underlying elections is that all members of a given group should be able to express their opinions simultaneously. Simultaneous primaries would provide a fairer test of opinion than a long-drawn-out process where the issues and candidates shift as returns from one state come to another which is preparing to vote.

Control by the voters over the delegates they send to conventions poses a difficult problem. As previously noted, in many states confusion arises because presidential primaries are used for the dual purpose of registering a choice among presidential candidates and electing delegates from local districts to conventions. Frequently the one function negatives the other. Overacker [Louise Overacker, *Presidential Primary,* 1926] suggests two ways of dealing with this problem. Under one plan, the preference vote would be eliminated and all delegates would be elected at large. Candidates for delegates would be listed on the ballot under the name of their presidential preference or as favoring an uninstructed delegation. Citizens would then have only one decision to make and one place on the ballot to mark.

A second plan would eliminate the vote for delegates and concentrate on the presidential preference. Names of presidential aspirants would be placed on the ballot at the request of five eligible voters, who would file with the secretary of state a list of delegates, equal to the total number to which the state was entitled, to represent the candidate in convention. The voter would indicate his choice among the aspirants or for an uninstructed delegation. After the primary, each presidential candidate would receive the same proportion of the whole delegation as he had received of the total vote cast. The secretary of state would then certify as elected the proper number of names from the lists filed with him, beginning at the top of the list. This plan, Overacker believes, would "secure a short ballot, proportional representation, a direct vote for a presidential candidate and responsibility for candidacies" [Charles E. Merriam and Louise Overacker, *Primary Elections,* 1928]. A variation of this proposal would give the candidate his proportionate share of the state's delegation, but the winning candidates themselves would select the delegates, thus assuring their loyalty in convention.

Most authorities on government have been agreed for some years that prospects for extending and strengthening the presidential primary system are not bright. On the other hand, it may be remembered that the presidential primary grew out of the deep split in the Republican party in the early years of the century, when the rank and file determined to exercise greater control over government. It may follow that the present schism between conservative and liberal elements in both major parties will bring a new demand for more direct participation by the voters in nomination of the men from whom they will choose the country's President.

HOW THE VOTER CAN HAVE HIS SAY [9]

Are you going to wait . . . till "the politicians" pick the candidates for President of the United States? Are you going to be content to choose . . . between two candidates picked for you by "the political machines"? The overwhelming answer from history is: You are!

You *could* help choose the candidates. You *could* help nominate your choice for President. . . .

In sixteen states of our Union there are primary elections in which you can make your influence felt in the choosing of delegates to the national conventions which, in turn, choose the presidential candidates. In most of the rest of the states delegates are chosen through party caucuses and state conventions. You are utterly welcome to vote in these primaries or to attend and vote in these caucuses. But—overwhelmingly—you do not.

Let me begin with my own state of Connecticut. It is basically a caucus-and-convention state. Local caucuses in 169 towns—free, open mass meetings of the local members of each party—choose delegates to a state convention; and the state convention chooses the delegates to the national convention. It is an indirect process; but it is a thoroughly workable one. Its effectiveness depends, however, on a good attendance at the local caucuses.

So what happens? In my town, in 1948, only about 10 per cent of the Republican voters came to the caucus. In the whole state the total attendance of Republicans at the Republican caucuses was about 15 per cent.

[9] From "This Year Help Nominate Your Presidential Candidate," by William Hard, senior editor, *Reader's Digest*. *Reader's Digest*. 60:14-18. February 1952. Reprinted by permission.

Is there not here a most deplorable abdication by the sovereign citizen of a vital part of his sovereignty?

Let us look at the state of Maryland, which holds primary elections for the selection of delegates to the state convention. I shall continue to use Republican figures. There is no contest at the time of writing for the Democratic nomination. At the November election in 1948 in Maryland there were 294,814 votes for the Republican presidential candidate, Dewey. But how many citizens had voted in the spring primary to choose state-convention delegates who would be for or against nominating Dewey as the Republican candidate? Only 17,854.

In New York State, as the result of a "reform," the voters vote directly for congressional district delegates to the national conventions. In each district the voters choose two delegates.

The 28th Congressional District of New York State is partly city, partly country, with a high level of civic intelligence. Its enrolled Republicans in 1948 were 74,657. Those who voted in the primary for delegates to the Republican national convention were 3903.

Why just denounce "the politicians"? Why not this year begin by denouncing yourself? And by getting busy in your party now?

In some states, like New Jersey, there has been another reform. The individual voter, in his party primary, can "write in" his individual personal choice for his party's presidential nomination. But see what this reform accomplishes in practice.

In New Jersey in 1948 in the November election the Republican presidential candidate got 981,124 votes. And how many Republicans in the spring primary had written in their individual personal preference for the Republican presidential nomination? Just 8976.

We need something more than better machinery for citizenship. We need better citizens.

In Illinois the machinery is quite wonderful. The voter in the primary can express his presidential preference either by a write-in or by voting for a name which has been put by petition on the ballot. But in Illinois there lives a Chicago hotelkeeper named Riley Alvin Bender who just loves running for the presidency. In

1948 he got himself on the primary ballot. He had no chance of getting a single vote in the Republican national convention. But what happened?

The Illinois Republican primary voters proceeded to vote right down "the regular line" on the ballot and they gave the practical joker, Mr. Bender, 324,029 presidential preference votes out of a total of 334,406.

That is how ridiculous the best voting machinery can become if the voters do not use their heads.

So how can we use our heads this year? How can we make ourselves felt in the choosing of our presidential candidates?

The first thing is: Get the facts about how your party in your state chooses its delegates to the national convention. . . . If [your local party leader] doesn't know, offhand, all the answers, ask him to get them for you. You will be serving notice that, this time, you are not going to surrender to him your right to help choose the candidates.

The second thing is: Join a local club organized in support of your candidate. If there isn't a club, start one.

A club in politics is a thing that is held over the heads of politicians and that makes a noise that is audible to them. There are thousands of such clubs already in existence, working hard for the nomination of various candidates. . . .

In this country all effective political power springs from the local grass roots and cobblestones.

So you and other members of your club will go about among your local politicians. What are politicians? Politicians are simply people who take more interest in public affairs than most people. Stop looking down on them. Take to yourself the memorable words uttered by Elihu Root, President Theodore Roosevelt's Secretary of State. He said:

"Politics in the practical exercise of the art of self-government. Somebody must attend to self-government if self-government is to continue. The principal reproach against any American should be that he is not a politician."

And rid yourself of another idea about politicians. A lot of people seem to think that the principal joy of politicians is to plant their flat feet on the necks of the voters. They are wrong.

The principal joy of politicians is to find candidates who will bring victory to their party. Politicians are absolutely open-minded toward ways to victory.

So, the next thing to do is: Make your club politically effective.

Tell your local politicians how strong your club is and how many members it contains. Invite them to come to your meetings and tell you how to get and support candidates in your local primary or caucus who will be favorable to your presidential favorite. . . .

Now get cars to take voters to the polls on caucus or primary day. And get baby-sitters to sit in women voters' homes, so that the women can go and vote. . . .

In your local caucus or primary your group may win. So also in your state conventions, if your state requires conventions. The history of such gatherings is filled with victories for voters who have convinced other voters—and politicians—that their candidate for the nomination for President is a winner.

But you may lose. Your state may perhaps not send to the national convention even *one* delegate pledged to vote for the nomination of your presidential favorite. That is when you really show what stuff you are made of. That is when you don't stop. That is when you keep going.

In every national convention there are many delegates who are "uninstructed." They are free to vote to nominate anybody. Many other delegates are "pledged." They are bound in honor—and sometimes in law—to vote for a certain man on the first ballot or on the first few ballots in the convention. But these pledged delegates can then switch—and always there are many of them who do switch—to somebody else.

Do not for a minute believe that everything in a national convention is sewed up from the start. That's a pernicious myth. . . . Keep thumping the tub and pounding the drum for your man till the national convention's very last ballot.

THE CAMPAIGN

EDITOR'S INTRODUCTION

Although radio and television have stimulated public interest in national conventions, it is actually with the presidential campaign that the political process begins to have a determining impact upon the voter. Present-day campaign methods are compared, in the opening article of this section, with those of the past. Next, a student of government discusses two possible types of campaign and in what circumstances each may be effective.

Do campaign speeches actually change votes? A public opinion survey, reported here, finds strong evidence that most voters make up their minds before hearing a single campaign speech and few change them. A warning is sounded, in another article, that the clamor of the presidential campaign should not drown out the appeals of candidates for Congress, who in the aggregate will have greater influence on the nation's policies than the Chief Executive.

A Washington correspondent who covered the 1952 presidential campaign finds that radio, television and the airplane, far from easing candidates' burdens, have increased these almost beyond human endurance. An editor, investigating the effectiveness of laws regulating campaign contributions and expenditures, finds these have produced chiefly a thriving crop of evasions. The cost of the 1952 campaign, it is suggested, may have reached the almost incredible total of $100 million. Means of combating these campaign evils are offered.

CAMPAIGNS LET OFF STEAM [1]

The earliest presidential candidates did not engage in campaigns. That was thought undignified. But by 1840—the year of W. H. Harrison's "log cabin and hard cider" campaign—the pattern was pretty well set. There have been changes in methods, to be sure—none more important that those introduced by the radio in 1924. But these are, after all, changes in degree rather than

[1] From "The Campaign—Our Political Safety Valve," by Henry Steele Commager, professor of history, Columbia University. *Senior Scholastic*. 53:15-16. October 6, 1948. Reprinted from Scholastic Magazines by permission of the editors.

in kind. There are the same speeches by the leading candidates, the same editorials and cartoons, the same mass meetings and parades, the same busy activity by the party organization—election posters, raising money, getting voters to register and to vote.

Far more than in other countries, American campaigns are concerned with candidates and personalities rather than with issues. This is partly because, in the United States, the voters elect the President. In countries that have the parliamentary system, people vote merely for members of the legislature who control the appointment of a prime minister.

Also, the American party system tends to ignore, or to confuse, issues. It is difficult to know which party to vote for on the mere matter of issues. (Which major party today stands for lowering the cost of living, for international cooperation, for preparedness, for opposing subversive influences? Obviously both.) Finally, in a country as large as ours, there are always dozens of local issues competing for attention. With a system of set elections every four years, moreover, there is always an accumulation of issues.

The major burden of any campaign falls upon the presidential candidates themselves. This burden used to be a very heavy one. Even with the radio, it is still a heavy one. It gravely taxes the strength of candidates, who are usually men past their prime. It cuts heavily into their time and the performance of their regular duties. Some candidates have refused to undertake this kind of campaigning. . . .

Perhaps it doesn't make much difference. Public opinion analysts are coming to believe what hard-boiled politicians have long believed: that few campaigns really change votes. Most people, they insist, have made up their minds well ahead of time.

Of course there is a large independent vote, but it ordinarily divides pretty evenly. Candidates and party organizations recognize this when they ignore certain states or sections and concentrate on others. It is only in states or regions where the vote is normally very close that it is worth a party's while to exert itself. And even there the real work is done not so much through speeches and parades, but by the local political organization in getting out the vote.

If all this is true, what is the use of an elaborate and long-drawn-out campaign?

This is really a double-barreled question. If we take the second part first, the answer is easy. There is no use in a long-drawn-out campaign. The tradition of a long campaign comes down to us from the prerailroad days and the preradio days. A hundred years or more ago it took months to get around the whole of the United States, to talk to people in every section and state. Nowadays, with rapid communication, a campaign can and should be conducted in a few weeks or a month. But traditions die hard, and the midsummer conventions and the fall campaigns will probably be with us for many years to come.

The first part of our question, though, is more important. What is the use of the campaign? The campaign has, in fact, many uses. The first, and most obvious, is that it educates the people politically. It serves to introduce the public to candidates and issues. It affords an opportunity for the thorough discussion of public affairs, and at a time when everyone is interested in the discussion. It forces the public to think about political questions, about national needs, and about the whole elaborate political machinery.

In the second place, it gives the American people a chance to blow off steam. It gives everyone a chance to say his say about policies and personalities, and gives every editor, every columnist, every cartoonist, every small-town politician, a chance to throw his weight around—temporarily. During campaigns Americans talk violently. They use the language of revolution and catastrophe. But once the election is over everyone goes about his business calmly enough. The campaign is the safety valve of American politics.

There is a third value, one that is so obvious that we are likely to take it for granted. Each campaign and election gives every American an object lesson in democracy, and brings every American into the democratic process as a participant. A national campaign is, in many respects, like a town meeting: everyone has his say. In the end, the individual casts his vote, and the majority of individual votes decides the issue. Americans know that every four years they will have a chance to decide on candidates and issues. They take pride in fulfilling this duty and responsibility.

The quadrennial campaign, then, is a pretty good thing. Yet it is subject to abuse. No one who studies American politics can doubt that it has been abused. There is too much talk about the Constitution and the Republic being at stake, too much viewing with alarm and pointing with pride, too much nonsense about the only parties that can save the country. A stenographic report of the things the average candidate—or even the average American—says during a campaign is enough to make any of us blush.

CARRYING THE CASE TO THE PEOPLE [2]

Perhaps the first question posed for candidates and their managers is the intensity of campaigning by the nominees themselves, often contrasted in the extreme by the terms "front porch" or "swing around the circle."

In the first case, the candidate does a limited amount of traveling and his workers carry the burden of the campaign. In a sense, this technique is the strategy of a superior position of an incumbent, a position gained by reason of a record known and commended to large numbers of voters. It has worked well for many nominees for local office.

On a national scale, Roosevelt in 1940 and 1944 attempted a stay-at-home campaign, pointing out that the war emergency was keeping him from the usual partisan campaign. On both occasions, however, the President ended by delivering a few speeches outside Washington, D.C. Herbert Hoover in 1932 likewise had to abandon, at least partially, his front-porch campaign. Many of his managers felt that his last-minute tour across the country was a case of too little and too late.

Nonincumbents Abraham Lincoln and William McKinley in their first presidential campaigns and Warren Harding in 1920

[2] From "Campaign Methods of Today," by Hugh A. Bone, professor of American government and policy, University of Washington. *Annals of the American Academy of Political and Social Science.* 283:127-40. September 1952. Reprinted by permission.

successfully used the front-porch technique. In each instance they were favored with certain fortuitous circumstances making speech-making and widespread appearances unnecessary. In each case the country was in a strong mood of protest against the incumbent party, and minor parties promised to siphon off what might normally be some Democratic votes. General Dwight Eisenhower was able to capture many delegates and voters in presidential primaries in the spring of 1952 by simply remaining on the job in Europe and leaving the management of his campaign to his supporters.

Most of the time, however, presidential candidates "ride the circuit" and make one to several cross-country tours. In certain of the larger doubtful and pivotal states a large number of appearances are made. Maine, Vermont and New Hampshire and those states south of Mason and Dixon's line are seldom favored with extensive appearances of presidential nominees. Often the candidate fails to make a single speech in those areas, on the theory that they are "safe" either for himself or for the opposition and that campaigning there will not change the outcome. . . .

A barnstorming campaign may be the only type holding any promise of success for an "unknown" or for an "underdog." Wendell Willkie, for example, was almost unknown, inasmuch as he had never before run for public office. It became necessary for him to "be seen" and get out and talk to the people. President Truman, though well known, entered the 1948 campaign as an "underdog" with virtually no one giving him any chance for election. His only hope seemed to rest with touring the country, making "whistle stops," and conducting a fighting campaign in language understood by the thousands who flocked to crossroads to see him in brief rear-platform appearances. It was indeed, as the New York *Times* phrased it, "a miracle of electioneering" based on an informal "off-the-cuff" style.

"Riding the circuit" probably helped Harry Truman to snatch victory from defeat and greatly aided Jackson in 1828, Wilson in 1912, and Roosevelt in 1932. On the other hand, the record-breaking barnstorming campaigns of Bryan and Willkie were unsuccessful. Neither the front porch nor the intensified campaign

is a sure thing. Conditions, the personality of the nominee, and
the nature of the opposition will govern the selection of one
strategy or the other. . . .

Another factor entering into over-all strategy is the balance
between offense and defense. Where an incumbent seeks reelection against an opponent who has little in his record to attack,
the incumbent will probably have to wage a defensive campaign.
For the party in power, sometimes attack is the best defense. In
1948 Democrats vigorously attacked the record of the Republican
Eightieth Congress; in fact, Truman made it the central issue of
the campaign. Governor Dewey, though having no connection
with this Congress, nonetheless was forced into a position of
having to run, at least in part, on its record. For a time Dewey
maneuvered Truman into a defensive position, but in the closing
days the President was able to get on the offensive with his attack on the Republicans in Congress.

To politicians, at least, the politics of protest offers promising strategy. This is based on the assumption that people would
rather vote against than for something—that a candidate's liabili-
ties are more important than his assets. They point to the pent-
up discontent against the Wilson and Hoover administrations as
the reason for their being voted out of office. Many popular
Democratic congressmen were retired in 1946 as a protest against
price controls, meat shortages, and other inconveniences. Undoubtedly protest is a formidable motivation, and it is sound
politics for the "outs" to center some of their fire on the party
in power. At the same time, it appears unproved as yet that a
purely negative approach is necessarily a winning one. Presidents
Roosevelt and Truman succeeded in campaigning on the basis
of positive programs already "delivered" or promised, which
benefited farmers, workers, and various minorities.

Numerous campaign managers believe in the wisdom of eva-
sion. In essence this means avoiding issues about which there is
sharp controversy and where to take a specific stand or position
might alienate blocs of voters. Campaign managers very carefully select the issues and often ghost-write speeches for their
nominees which deal in the most general terms. To a consider-

able extent Wilson's "New Freedom" and Roosevelt's "New Deal" were first spelled out in general language, and the Dewey-Warren "unity" campaign likewise avoided being too specific. Many observers felt that this method was the reason for the latter's defeat, especially when Mr. Truman countered by specifically endorsing measures in which certain groups were interested.

In many respects the principle underlying campaign methods and strategy is that campaigns cannot be based upon principles. Broadly speaking, campaign arguments grow out of the political and economic environment of the moment, the character of the nominees themselves, and the imagination of their managers. There are, however, two or three "reliables" or issues considered perennial and axiomatic. An incumbent will probably warn or attempt to raise fears of the danger of changes. For over a hundred years, the challenger has campaigned against the "extravagance" and "bureaucracy" of the party in power. Both sides usually employ "guilt by association" techniques. Republicans are associated with "Wall Street" and moneyed lobbies, and Democrats with Socialists and left-wing labor leaders. Beyond this, the key words in campaign management are flexibility, adaptability, resourcefulness, and opportunism.

DO CAMPAIGNS CHANGE VOTES? [3]

For thirteen years the American Institute of Public Opinion, through its continuous polling, has been collecting information on the voting behavior of the American people. During three presidential campaigns and innumerable state and local contests our interviewers have talked with scores of thousands of voters in all walks of life—farmers, factory workers, housewives, businessmen, white-collar workers and all other major voting groups. These surveys provide a picture of how Americans react politically, and why.

[3] From an article by George Gallup and William A. Lydgate of the American Institute of Public Opinion. *Saturday Evening Post.* 221:23+. July 3, 1948. Copyright 1948, by the Curtis Publishing Company. Reprinted by permission.

Do platforms really influence voters? . . .

Three weeks after publication of the Republican platform of 1944, we conducted a coast-to-coast poll to find out how many people had read it. We found that only about one third had read any part of the document, and even fewer could remember anything that it said. Only one in ten knew what the platform said about America's postwar role in world affairs. Only one farmer in twelve could remember anything it said about agriculture. Only one worker in sixteen was familiar with any part of the platform dealing with labor or jobs.

A similar test in 1940 found that even fewer voters had bothered to read anything in the GOP platform on which Wendell Willkie ran or the platform which Franklin D. Roosevelt used in his historic bid for a third term.

An outrageously bad platform might lose some votes, and a phenomenally good one might win some. But, on the whole, it may be doubted that platforms play a very significant role in attracting votes when so few people know what is in them. In a way, it is a tribute to the intelligence of the people that they don't pay much attention to platforms. Parties are sometimes trapped by their own patently insincere platform promises and kept from doing the right thing. However, platforms do serve the purpose of giving party workers a consistent set of arguments to use in the campaign. Otherwise their efforts would inevitably be tangled in contradiction—from state to state and district to district. Most political observers agree that platforms still serve this purpose adequately.

Do presidential campaigns change votes? Politicians are apt to think that many voters start off a campaign with completely open minds, ready to listen to campaign arguments, weigh the evidence and then make up their minds how to vote. Maybe that's how we should behave. But it isn't the way we do behave. In a very real sense, presidential campaigns are over before they begin. [This was written before the campaign of 1948, in which it was generally agreed that President Truman turned the tide in his favor by his aggressive whistle-stop tour of the nation.—Ed.]

They are decided to a great extent by events that have occurred in the entire period between two presidential elections, rather than by the campaign. In politics it is always later than you think.

Of course, it would be foolish to claim that campaigns have no effect or change no votes. But they appear to have less effect and to change fewer votes than the average party leader would like to think. Voters listen to campaigns pretty largely to confirm what they already think.

In 1940 our poll found as early as May that 57 per cent of the nation's voters were planning to vote for Roosevelt for a third term. Nobody knew at that time whom the Republicans would nominate. The convention which named Wendell Willkie did not meet until June. On Election Day, six months later, Roosevelt got 55 per cent.

In 1944 the country made up its mind even earlier and there was even less net change. A presidential "trial-heat" race between Roosevelt and Dewey which the Gallup Poll conducted in April 1944, found Roosevelt polling 55 per cent, Dewey 45 per cent. On Election Day, in November, the vote divided 54 per cent to 45 per cent. There were some shifts of sentiment back and forth in the intervening period, but the net shift was small. But some interesting questions are raised by those facts. . . .

A big question mark about the effect of presidential campaigns was raised by a public-opinion study in 1940 in Erie County, Ohio. Paul Lazarsfeld, of Columbia University, and Elmo Roper, director of the Fortune Poll, conducted a series of seven monthly surveys in the county between May and November. At the start, in May, they found a solid Republican majority. This increased only slightly in the course of the campaign. By June, before the presidential race really got started, 80 per cent of the voters of Erie county had made up their minds how they were going to vote, and never changed them during the course of the campaign. This left 20 per cent who hesitated long enough to be considered at least theoretically susceptible to campaign propaganda. But Lazarsfeld reported that in the end these people divided about the same way as the rest, so that the ratio of Democratic and Republican voting intentions which existed when the campaign began was not altered by the campaign.

Does this mean that a political party could give up campaigning and win? Probably not. Some kind of campaign would be needed to keep in line the voting intentions of those who do make up their minds early, Lazarsfeld concluded.

Yet in presidential races today, everything is made to depend on the campaign—as if the voters lived in a mental vacuum for three and a half years and only snapped out of it between June and November of the fourth year. Is this wise—this pitching of all effort and money into a campaign and then coasting along for four years? Perhaps political leaders could profitably spend more time trying to increase public acceptance of their party between elections.

Maybe campaigns would influence people more if they were not fought on such an incredibly low plane. Candidates abandon all pretense of sportsmanship, fairness or intelligence. They set up straw men and knock them over. They call the opponents blackguards and liars, and they try to outvie them in attempting to bribe minority groups with promises. Is it surprising that we voters don't fall for this vituperation and double-talk?

Apparently we've remained impervious to it for a good many decades. After studying our political ways, [British Ambassador James] Bryce sixty years ago concluded that campaigns influence few people. The following passage from *The American Commonwealth* might easily describe any modern presidential campaign:

> Anyone who should read the campaign literature of the Republicans would fancy that they were opposed to the Democrats on many important points. When he took up the Democratic speeches and pamphlets, he would again be struck by the serious divergences between the parties, which, however, would seem to arise, not on points raised by the Republicans, but on other points which the Republicans had not referred to. . . . Each pummels, not his true enemy, but a stuffed figure set up to represent that enemy. . . .

> What impression do these appeals and discussions make upon the voters? Comparatively little.

Do speeches change many votes? The common strategy of election-campaign managers when they think a certain state is doubtful is to dispatch the candidate there to make a rousing speech and pull things into line. But in the course of thirteen years of polling, covering more than 190 state, local and national elections, we have found little evidence that one speech or even a series of speeches changes many votes. . . .

We have tested political opinion just before a candidate arrives in a state for a speaking tour, and again after he has left. The difference is almost always negligible.

Alfred E. Smith created a sensation in January 1936, with his famous "take-a-walk" speech, breaking dramatically with his friend and protégé, Roosevelt. Denouncing the New Deal, Smith invited the country to repudiate Roosevelt in November. While every politician in the country was excitedly discussing what this rupture might mean to the President's chances of re-election, we polled the country and found that Roosevelt had gained 1 per cent in popularity.

The theory that one prominent man can swing blocs of votes: party henchmen are jubilant if they can persuade a big mogul of labor, or an important farm leader, or a religious figure to endorse their candidate. The theory is that the followers of such a key man will likely go where he leads politically.

But will they? The evidence is by no means uniform. People don't necessarily vote in blocs because a leader tells them to, no matter how much they may respect the leader for other things. There no doubt are times when leader endorsement does change votes; it would depend both on the type of leader and the nature of the group. But, in general, when a given group of voters makes up its mind where its interests lie, it will vote according to those interests regardless of whether a leader of the group urges such a vote or opposes it. Some of the credit that is given to leaders of unions, farm organizations and other groups for swinging their followers in an election may be unwarranted.

To cite one example, John L. Lewis failed utterly to influence the members of the CIO when he bolted the Democratic ranks in 1940. Lewis, the founder of the CIO, rejected Roosevelt and supported Willkie. As the campaign drew to a close, Lewis proclaimed that if Roosevelt won he, Lewis, would resign from the CIO. And he did. After the election, when the American Institute of Public Opinion polled CIO members, asking them how they had voted in the election, 79 per cent said they had favored Roosevelt. Even in the Pennsylvania mining area Lewis' action made little difference in the vote.

Newspaper editorials also seem to have little influence in swinging votes: witness Roosevelt's string of reelections in the face of opposition from an overwhelming proportion of the press. The Chicago *Tribune* is credited with having considerable influence in Chicago. Although it fulminated against the Roosevelt Administration with increasing fury, Cook County (Chicago) was one of the few areas in the country which actually showed an increase in Roosevelt's strength between 1940 and 1944. Cook County voted Democratic by 55½ per cent in 1940 and by 58 per cent four years later. . . .

How decisive is the influence of political machines? The power of political machines was greatest when our cities teemed with immigrants newly arrived from Europe. Many were uneducated, illiterate, totally ignorant of American customs and political issues. The machines, undertaking the political education of the newcomers, herded them to the polls to vote the straight ticket. Today, things are a bit different. Mass education and mass communication have given the immigrant and his descendants a greater independence of thought. . . .

In the last two presidential elections, contiguous states with political machines varying greatly in efficiency voted almost exactly the same way. It is hard to reconcile this fact with the theory that machines are decisive in national elections. Certainly no one would claim that the Democratic machines in Massachusetts, New Hampshire, Connecticut, New York, New Jersey, Pennsylvania, Ohio, Michigan, Indiana, Illinois, Wisconsin and Minnesota are approximately equal in potency or importance. Yet, in that whole band of states, stretching across the northern half of the nation, the Democratic vote showed a variation of only a few percentage points from state to state in both the 1940 and 1944 presidential elections. When a state in which a party's machine activity is feeble and spasmodic votes the same way as an adjoining state where the same party's machine is vigorous, one wonders how much credit machines can claim. . . .

Machines are powerful, however, in two types of elections —primaries and local elections. In local elections they can control nominations and hence decide for whom the voters must vote. In primaries, voter apathy usually is high. By getting out a well-organized portion of the party vote, machines can influence the outcome. As a cynic once crudely pit it, "Machines are most effective when voters don't give a damn who wins."

The women's-vote-myth. A tip to . . . presidential candidates: Don't worry too much about the women's vote or "how to win the women over." They don't vote in a bloc, and they don't vote differently from men. . . .

This can be seen by examining the vote cast by men and by women for any given candidate in a presidential election. The division of sentiment among women is almost identical with that among men. Rarely in recent years has it amounted to more than two percentage points. That is, if the male vote for the country goes Democratic by say 54 per cent, the feminine Democratic vote will, on the average, be within two percentage points of that figure.

The reason seems to be that, on political matters, women generally accept the judgment of their menfolk. They take their cue from the opinions or prejudices of a husband, a father, a son or other male member of the family. Of course, this is not true of all women. But in the average household the woman goes on the theory that her man knows more about those things than she does. Polls have found that when a change of political sentiment takes place, it almost always starts with the men, not the women. The women catch up with the trend later—after they've talked to the boss.

In all fairness, it should be said that there is no real reason why women should vote differently from men, even if they paid no attention to the ideas of the allegedly dominant male. No one would argue that women ought to vote differently just for the sake of being different. The only point here is that one must be cautious in talking about the woman's viewpoint in politics. Although the average male candidate running for office usually makes quite an effort to win the feminine vote, it may be questioned whether such pains are necessary. If male voters can be won over, the women will generally come along too.

The myth of the band-wagon vote. The band-wagon theory presupposes that many voters behave like sheep, that they will hasten to join the side that seems likely to prevail. The theory leads to absurdities when, in the closing days of a campaign, each national chairman solemnly boasts that his candidate is going to lick the daylights out of the opponent. But the theory back of it is all false. Voters don't behave according to the band-wagon psychology.

If there is such a thing as a band-wagon vote, then the candidates who are ahead in an election campaign must inevitably increase their lead. If they do not, then there can be no such thing as a band-wagon vote. But in the course of conducting election polls and of measuring opinion on public issues, we have never found any common tendency for the more popular candidate to improve his position or the more popular side of an issue to gain strength—a situation required by the band-wagon theory. Indeed, the fact is that the trends never seem to follow any consistent pattern. Sometimes there is a downward trend for the leading candidate, sometimes an upward trend, and sometimes no trend at all. For example:

Thomas E. Dewey took an early lead of 54 per cent in the first Institute poll of the 1942 governorship race in New York State. According to the band-wagon theory, the Dewey percentage should have risen in subsequent polls as the voters, noting Dewey ahead—he also led in the New York *Daily News* poll —climbed on the band-wagon of the winner. But what happened? In six succeeding surveys the net change in the Dewey vote was exactly 1 per cent, and it was a loss of 1 per cent, at that. The final report gave Dewey 53 per cent, and he won with exactly 53 per cent in the election. . . .

In national elections we always poll voters on the question, "Regardless of how you yourself plan to vote, who do you think will win?" The results consistently reveal a very large percentage of voters planning to vote for the side they think will lose. If the band-wagon theory is correct, then the number of people who voted for Roosevelt should have been at least approximately the same as those who thought he would win, since, according to the theory, they would want to climb on his band-wagon. But no such relationship existed. In 1944, for instance, a total of 74 per cent thought Roosevelt would win, but only 53.8 per cent voted for him.

And so it goes, for a picture which decidedly fails to indicate any pattern consistent with the band-wagon theory.

If speeches, platforms, campaigns, party activity, and so on, don't seem to affect many voters, what does influence them? How do they make up their minds?

As already indicated, events between elections have a good deal of influence. The impact of events is greatest on the minds of independent voters.

Habit plays a big part, too—millions vote for the same party during their entire lifetime. It makes little difference to these die-hards who the candidates are or what the issues are. Their behavior is typified by the remark of one voter: "I vote for the best man, but the best man is always a Democrat." Lancaster County, South Carolina, can almost always be counted on to vote 99 per cent Democratic—in 1936 it actually voted Democratic by 100 per cent. On the other hand, Johnson County, Tennessee, votes 85 per cent Republican come hell, high water or Warren G. Harding.

The tendency of many of us to stick habitually to one party during a whole lifetime doubtless is bad. Democracy would be a lot healthier if we all showed more independence in our political thinking. In choosing parties and sticking to them, we follow a sort of instinct of self-interest. We adhere to a party because we've convinced ourselves that that is the party most concerned with our welfare. The lifelong Democrat is the man who is deeply convinced that only the Democrats are adequately looking out for his plight. It is natural for a man to want to vote for a party he considers sympathetic to his problems, although there may not always be much logic in his choice. The problem of winning elections is how to make the majority feel that your side is more sympathetic to their welfare than the other party is.

The Republican party went into the doghouse in 1932 because many low-income voters lost faith in its ability to champion the interests of the poor. Repeatedly after 1932, polls by the Gallup organization found that voters considered the GOP the best party for people of above-average income, but that the Democrats were best for people of average and below-average income. All the speeches and platforms and campaigns of the Republicans could not erase that impression from the minds of the voters, the majority of whom felt that the actions of the Republican party were more in the interests of the privileged few than of the broad masses. Since the masses have the votes, the Republicans had to struggle against terrific odds.

CONGRESS IS IMPORTANT, TOO [4]

As the delegates gather again [for the 1952 national conventions], we are once more impressed by the illusory character of the American political battle. . . . After the nominations have been made, by whatever deals behind the scenes, the campaign will be fought out in terms of these nominees. Four years ago this meant that the voters were asked to believe that Mr. Dewey was the incarnation of the Republican cause and Mr. Truman of the Democratic. Both men, with their supporters, campaigned on this assumption. "Dewey" equated "Republican"; "Truman" equated "Democratic."

As a matter of fact, as every thinking American knew, neither equation was truthful or honest. Governor Dewey did not represent the "rock-ribbed Republicanism" of such party leaders as McCarthy, Bricker, Capehart, Jenner or Colonel Robert R. McCormick. Since that election Senator Taft has had to defend

[4] From "The Optical Illusion of Politics," editorial. *Christian Century.* 69:774. July 2, 1952. Reprinted by permission.

himself against the charge that his desire for a Dewey victory was so tepid that on the morning after the surprising outcome, he wrote a congratulatory letter to President Truman. No more did Mr. Truman represent the Democratic majority, as the subsequent record in Congress has shown. He has never been able to count on party support either for many policies advocated in his 1948 platform or for many of the things he promised those whose votes he was seeking. The party conflict four years ago, in other words, was largely an optical illusion.

It was an illusion created by the concentration of public attention on the two presidential candidates. For the presidential contest is only one part of the quadrennial battle at the polls, and it is not the most important part. Equally important, and often—as subsequent events prove—more important, is the election of Congress. . . . Party labels no longer mean much of anything in those two bodies. And no matter how wise may be the policies advocated by the . . . Chief Executive, if he cannot induce Congress to vote for them, his administration will be a failure.

Yet what happens in the election of members of the Congress of the United States? All sorts of local interests and prejudices control most of the nominations and elections. There are parts of the country where scores of senators and representatives are renominated and elected out of sheer habit. Years of handshaking, back-slapping, letter-writing, baby-kissing and barbecue-attending pay off with all but automatic reelections. Issues, save of the most local sort, never enter into the picture. In other districts that peculiar but potent American institution, "the courthouse gang," sees to it that congressional seats are kept as a reward for faithful service. And one can count by the hundred the senators and congressmen whose terms are an award for ability in logrolling post offices or army camps or dams or other federal adornments of the local landscape.

Here in fact is one spot at which our system of government is most in danger of breaking down. The American citizen, as he exercises his sovereign powers to choose his own rulers, again and again is beguiled into frustration by this political illusion.

Well-intentioned voters who . . . become absorbed in the presidential canvass . . . [and] work their heads off for their preferred presidential candidate . . . complacently accept for the vacant congressional post in their state or district some party hack who, if he gets to Washington, will do everything in his power to sabotage and ruin the policies of that same candidate. The process makes no sense. It reduces the operations of federal government to chaos and continual confusion. Yet it goes on all the while. . . .

So watch the . . . national conventions with the concentrated attention they deserve. They are the greatest show on earth, and any time the citizen spends listening to the radio reports, looking at the television images, reading the columns which the press will devote to what happens off stage and on, will be time well spent. But while the citizen watches the unfolding drama . . . any intelligent concern for the nation's welfare . . . [trusts] that he will not be fooled by it. For no matter who is nominated . . . the nation's future, especially in its relations with the rest of the world, will largely depend on the composition of the . . . Congress. It is there that civic responsibility becomes most local, most inescapable. It is there that the struggle for intelligent government can most easily be lost.

ARE CAMPAIGNS TOO TOUGH? [5]

The one thing on which both the winner and loser were agreed during and after . . . [the 1952 presidential campaign] was that this was the most exhausting election on record and that there must be a better way to do the job. . . .

The main complaints on which most observers on the two campaign trains agreed were as follows:

1. It lasted too long. It not only exhausted every idea the candidates had weeks before it was finished and became a definite menace to their health, but it paralyzed policy over much of the

[5] From "Our Campaign Techniques Reexamined," by James Reston, New York *Times* diplomatic correspondent. New York *Times Magazine*. p8+. November 9, 1952. Reprinted by permission.

free world for a period of at least five months. (Not counting the hard month of campaigning before the Republican convention, General Eisenhower made 228 speeches and covered just under 50,000 miles; and Governor Stevenson made 203 speeches and traveled 32,500 miles.)

2. It cost too much money—estimates range up to $82 million. Thus it gave an unfair advantage to the side that could raise the most money and it increased the possibility of poor government, for the rule of politics usually is "the larger the kick-in, the larger the pay-off."

3. It did not use television as a means of giving the candidates more time for reflection and an easier opportunity of reaching the people. It merely imposed the television routine on top of the usual routine, which was already a menace to the sanity of the candidates and the patience of the voters.

4. The airplane contributed to the strain, too. This mode of transportation, added to the campaign trains and the motorcades, meant that the candidates went more places, and were constantly pushing their way through crowds from plane, to motorcade, to train. . . .

5. It was a one-way campaign—even more so than in the past—because the candidates raised questions in their speeches which they never answered. The speeches tended to become a series of debating points, but the people had no means of getting back at the candidates with their questions, for the press conference was abandoned almost as soon as the campaign started.

In summary the method of electing a President is getting out of hand. The struggle for power is becoming so fierce that the candidates are not only jeopardizing their strength, but saying things which they do not always mean and which divide the nation, mislead its allies and its enemies, and thus make the winner's task of governing more difficult when he finally reaches the White House. . . .

When a campaign goes on as long, and covers as much distance as this one did, several things inevitably happen. The first thing that happens is that the candidates not only get tired but they get overwhelmed by the schedule. They cannot produce speeches fast enough to meet the next stop and are therefore forced more and more to mouth the writings and ideas of other men, or to adopt a series of debating points which they repeat like actors on a vaudeville circuit.

No presidential candidate of our time actually wrote so many speeches or so many good speeches as Governor Stevenson: not Franklin Roosevelt nor even the Governor's own personal hero, Woodrow Wilson. The speeches will be collected and passed on for years as a model. But even Mr. Stevenson, who . . . worked eighteen hours a day . . . [from] the middle of September, was not able to do more after the first of October than add a paragraph here and a peroration there to the work of other men.

The idea persisted to the end that he was writing all his own speeches, but it wasn't true. The soaring speech he delivered in the Mormon Tabernacle in Salt Lake City—probably the noblest document of the campaign—was almost entirely the work of Herbert Agar, the former editor of the Louisville *Courier-Journal* who now lives in England.

The shrewd and moving address he produced in Richmond, Virginia, was almost entirely the work of David Cohn, the freelance writer from the Mississippi delta via New Jersey. And throughout the campaign, he drew upon memoranda from probably the most brilliant stable of writers ever gathered together in a presidential campaign; Arthur Schlesinger Jr., Archibald MacLeish, Bernard DeVoto and Kenneth Galbraith of the Harvard faculty; Robert E. Sherwood, the playwright, and Judge Samuel Rosenman, formerly on the speech-writing staff of President Roosevelt; James Wechsler, editor of the New York *Post*; and David Bell and Clayton Fritchey, who headed the White House staff working in Springfield, Illinois.

General Eisenhower did not even attempt to write his own speeches or contribute much to them, even at the beginning. He relied, not on the Harvard faculty but on the staffs of the big Eastern magazines for his scripts—Stanley High from the *Reader's Digest*, Gabriel Hauge from *Business Week*, C. D. Jackson from *Time* and Emmet Hughes from *Life* for almost all his prepared addresses.

And the point of this is not that this was wrong, but that it was inevitable, and that it could lead to a situation where the most impressive candidate in a presidential race is not the man who has the most to say out of his heart and mind to the voters, but the man who can put together the best team of speech writers and buy the most time on the national television hook-ups.

Television can be a great equalizer in a presidential campaign. It can, for example, enable a man such as Stevenson, who was not well known last July when he was nominated, to expose his ideas and his personality from coast to coast before Election Day and thus to minimize the advantage of an opponent who may happen to start with such a national reputation as Eisenhower's. . . .

It is possible to imagine an election . . . in which one side would have so much more money than the other side that it could buy enough TV time to unbalance the election and maybe even—as the Democrats charged in the late madness—to "saturate" the air in certain key areas with campaign propaganda for one candidate.

More likely, and in some ways more dangerous, is the possibility that the campaigns have already become so expensive that the new President will be more and more under obligation to those who raise or contribute the most money. It may be easy for a new President to turn down a candidate for ambassadorship who contributed several hundred, or even several thousand, dollars to the campaign, or to be unaffected by the appeals of labor leaders who raise much more, but when the sums to be raised reach into the tens of millions, and when the President, as party leader, has to look forward to another campaign where he will want to go back for more millions, then the whole question of money-raising and policy-making and appointment-making are likely to get more and more mixed up.

It was thought a year or so ago that both the nation-wide TV hook-up and the airplane were going to make campaigning easier, but in some ways the opposite has been the effect. Those who had those fond dreams imagined that maybe the candidates would make a few major speeches, via the coaxial cable, perhaps flying to various regions of the country to originate these major gems of political policy and philosophy. But nothing so simple or sensible seems to be developing.

Instead, the airplane and the TV camera, like so many modern "conveniences," have not simplified but have merely complicated life. Both were merely superimposed on top of the old-fashioned back-platform whistle-stop routine, so that these two new straws may very well be the ones to break the candidate's back. . . .

Even four or eight years ago, it was always possible for the candidate to tell the senator from New Mexico that his fondest hope was to go to Albuquerque to campaign for that senator's reelection, but that time and distance did not permit a special trip to Albuquerque. . . .

The modern presidential nominee, however, is now robbed of his excuse. He can fly to Albuquerque these days in a few hours, and the senator won't take "no" for an answer. . . .

Consequently, the candidates now do what Stevenson and Eisenhower did all through the month of October. They knock themselves out trying to keep peace in the party. They fly thousands of miles because it is physically possible to do so and because the senator will be sore if they don't. But, meanwhile, they impose on themselves a strain that defies common sense and forces them into the kind of endurance contest just ended.

When the President was elected in November and didn't take office until March, the winner had time to rest and recover his health and poise before jumping into the punishing routine of his job but . . . [last year's] champion has not only had to put up with the new rigors of the modern campaign; he had to take office on January 21.

This means that within eleven weeks he had to try to recover, pick up the pieces of the campaign, undo all the damage caused at home and abroad by all those overstatements, all those personal attacks and all those slick debating points—and meanwhile pick a cabinet, organize a personal staff, find out what is going on in the world, supervise the budget for Congress and thank all the people who wrote in to say that his election was the greatest thing since the days of General Washington.

All these things are further complicated by the fact that the modern campaign is tending more and more to use not only the airplane, the TV and other forms of rapid communication, but to rely on the techniques of modern salesmanship—a fact which encourages the candidates to try to "put over" their arguments without giving the people much chance to answer back. . . .

The net of this procedure is that the one candidate tends to put out whatever he thinks will be effective, and the other candidate answers back, usually putting just as much spin on his answer as his opponent did on the original statements, so that the voters are left with two widely divergent views of the facts without any means of getting at the real truth of the question at issue. . . .

In short, the *excuse* for abandoning the old habit of responding to questions is that there is no time, but the *reason* is that the candidates find it more convenient to plan what they want to say and put out what they think will be most effective, without the embarrassment of having to answer the questions they themselves raise.

What can be done about all this? The answer is that we probably cannot do much, because the struggle for power is fierce and politicians are not noted for abiding by the rules. Several things, however, may at least be worth considering.

1. All laws governing campaign expenditures should be reviewed before 1956 by a bipartisan or nonpartisan commission, for the present laws are now an obvious joke. Both parties have found innumerable ways to evade them. For example, while the laws limit the amount of money any individual can "give" to a campaign fund, the device of "lending" money to the national committees enables a well-heeled patron to hand over as much as he likes and then to cancel it off as a "bad debt" on his income tax returns.

Also, by the simple expedient of creating additional committees, such as the Volunteers for Stevenson, or the Citizens for Eisenhower, it is permissible under present laws to raise additional millions of dollars for campaign purposes.

2. On the question of television, which is the new factor in the equation which is pushing campaign expenditures to the danger point, one idea might be to limit the number of national TV broadcasts by agreement between the parties, to, say seven or eight. Another would be to have the television networks con-

tribute the time for these fourteen or sixteen half hours as—to use their favorite phrase—"public service." . . .

3. The good old-fashioned American habit of political heckling should be revived at least to a certain extent. There is nothing in the Constitution which requires the people to listen like dolts to obvious falsehoods and half-truths which are recognized as such by at least some of the people in every audience. It wouldn't take many well-timed but just outcries from a few political audiences to make the candidates a little more cautious.

4. The press conference should be revived during the campaign. If all the candidates were approached by the press, radio and TV organizations before they were nominated, it would not be difficult to get a flat commitment to hold a weekly news conference during the campaign. And if this were accepted, the candidates again would be a little more careful with the truth.

5. Finally, if we are going to go on being this tough on our presidential candidates—and we probably are—the least we can do is to take a little more care about the way in which we pick our vice-presidential candidates. Both Senators Nixon and Sparkman were picked this year in accordance with the tradition—without a thought to the idea that Presidents do die, and that even Lincoln was shot.

DO CAMPAIGNS COST TOO MUCH? [6]

For the past several months we conducted an intensive investigation to determine exactly how much the American people pay every four years to put a man of their choice into the White House. . . .

From a variety of sources, both official and unofficial, we were able to work out the over-all pattern of campaign spending.

This pattern brings out one paramount fact: that it costs more to elect the President of the United States than it does to choose or install any other official in the world. On the basis of reports filed under the Hatch Act (and we shall presently explain why

[6] From "What Price Presidents?" by Serge Fliegers, contributing editor, *American Mercury.* *American Mercury.* 75:20-31. October 1952. Reprinted by permission.

this is but a fraction of the total outlay), the cost to Americans of returning Truman to the White House was $13,563,878. Meanwhile, in England, Winston Churchill was returned to Parliament with an expenditure of $2,234.40 (£798).

Though the comparison isn't a fair one—Churchill was campaigning only for his own safe seat in the House—these two figures do give some idea of the relative cost of electioneering on both sides of the Atlantic. The real story of the election of a President, however, involves not only the question of how much money it costs, but—most important—where that money comes from and where it goes.

The Hatch Act requires filing of receipts and expenses by political organizations operating across state lines and in general elections only. Thus we know, for example, that the Democratic National Committee spent $2,127,296 during the last election, and the Republican National Committee spent $2,736,334. The Democratic Senatorial Campaign Committee, during the same time, spent $49,273, while its Republican counterpart invested $500,254 in a victory that remained elusive. . . .

But what of the innumerable local committees that collected and spent thousands of dollars during the campaign? Their figures are not on the record. Nor are the amounts spent in primaries—such as the Texas campaign which reputedly cost Senator Connally $1,500,000 or the Ohio campaign in which Taft was helped by $1,808,000.

Political scientists specializing in the field of campaign finance, and the acting treasurer of one national politcal committee, gave us independent estimates of what the true cost of a campaign amounts to, including the sums spent in primaries and by local committees not required to file statements. They agreed that this amounts to approximately ten times the amount reported under the Hatch Act.

That would bring the cost of the 1948 campaign up to $130 million. And the estimates for . . . [the 1952] campaign would come close to the quarter-billion mark. . . .

It was Mark Hanna, working for McKinley, who first had the bright idea that presidential elections could be turned into big business. He approached all banks and corporations operating under Federal charter and virtually leveled an assessment on their profits. This brought him over $3 million and the undying hatred of bankers and corporate lawyers. As a result of Hanna's high-handedness, legislation was later passed prohibiting political contributions from banks and corporations. (Some firms which helped push through this law now spend as much time thinking up ways to circumvent it in order to help the candidate of their choice.)

But even with corporate millions officially out of the way, election costs have kept climbing quadrennially. Even during the depression, when Americans were clutching their money in a tight fist, they decided to relax their grip on 5,146,000 dollar bills in order to bring Roosevelt to Washington. . . .

Roosevelt brought three new developments to the old game.

Although it seemed insignificant at the time, Roosevelt's most far-reaching action took place when he introduced electronics into elections. People were mostly amused when he started his fireside chats. Today, the air waves carry an unending stream of political material, from the radio spot announcements of the local candidate to the week-long TV coverage of national conventions. And the cost of radio and TV has become indisputably the major item in today's election budget.

Partly stemming from Roosevelt's use of the radio and other mass communication media, and partly because Roosevelt managed to drive his campaign to a height of dramatic intensity, there came a second development: more people listened and voted than ever before. A little better than three million people cast their ballot in the campaign between Lincoln and Douglas. Thirty-seven million voted when Roosevelt made his first bid for the White House. And close to fifty million men and women went to the polls during Roosevelt's last contest. . . .

A third factor to enter politics during Roosevelt's tenure of office was the strong hand of labor. Prior to the depression, Samuel Gompers' interdict on labor meddling in general politics had been strictly heeded by union leaders. But Roosevelt negotiated an alliance with labor, and with the 1940 campaign the CIO's Political Action Committee had definitely become a *troisième force*, strong enough to place Henry Wallace on the Roosevelt ticket.

Much as a result of these three developments, and the intensity of the 1940 campaign which really frightened legislators, Congress amended, assembled, and issued new laws regulating election practices. The old Federal Corrupt Practices Act was augmented by the Hatch Act and later by the Smith-Connally and the Taft-Hartley laws. This legislation was designed to put a fence around what Dr. Ralph M. Goldman calls the Big Three of American politics: Big Business, Big Labor, and Big Government.

As it stands today, this legislation is supposed to limit Big Business by establishing a $3 million a year top on the expenditure of a committee, and a $5,000 top on individual contributions.

Banks, corporations, and public utilities cannot contribute at all.

Candidates may not spend more than $5,000 to campaign for a seat in the House of Representatives, not more than $25,000 to seek the privilege of occuying a high-backed chair in the Senate.

Big Government is strictly banned from campaign activities. Government employees may not be coerced, solicited, or otherwise influenced by their bosses. Nor may a member of the executive branch take an active part in any political campaign.

Big Labor is also required to stay out of politics. Union funds may not be directly used in general elections, nor may union members be assessed for political purposes. . . .

It was Roosevelt again who had the first idea of how to nullify the $3 million limitation of the Hatch Act. "If each committee can only spend $3 million—well then, let's have many committees." It was as brilliant as it was simple.

In the last campaign before the Hatch Act went into effect, the Democrats had spent $5,194,741 and the Republicans $8,892,-972. Now Roosevelt invented the "independent" committee, and they flourished overnight, from Hollywood (Samuel Goldwyn Southern California Committee for Roosevelt) to Ossining, New York (Ossining Independent Citizens for Roosevelt Committee). All these "independent" groups collected and spent an approximate aggregate of $50 million during the first election after passage of the Hatch Act limitation. Today, there are 144 independent groups, and some—such as the Citizens for Eisenhower Committee—have managed to elbow their way to a place equal in importance with the regular party organization.

In some respects, this intrusion of amateurs into politics is one of the healthiest developments we have seen during the past few years. But, as regards electoral financing, these groups only serve to complicate the picture and increase the cost of elections. Efforts are duplicated and overhead costs for headquarters, staff, mailing and publicity are often tripled. . . .

If legislators were naive enough to believe that their provision limiting individual contributions to $5,000 per year would restrict the openhandedness of political enthusiasts, they have a rude shock coming to them.

They might be interested to learn that the late Mr. Lammot du Pont . . . gave a total of $31,322.79 to twelve different Republican outfits during the 1944 elections. The total contribution of the du Pont family reached the phenomenal sum of $109,-832.83. Next largest Republican contributors were the Pew oil family of Pennsylvania with $96,995.76, the Mellons with $59,-500 and the Rockefellers with $52,400.

Rich friends of the Democrats made up in enthusiasm what they lacked in lavishness. Samuel Goldwyn and his wife sent checks totaling $13,250. Mr. and Mrs. Marshall Field and young Stanley came through with $22,500, while the Higgins boat-building family, having amassed a fortune making Liberty ships for the government, encouraged the party in power to the tune of $20,000.

Why do these people pay out such enormous sums to support their candidate? In many instances, it is a matter of principle. They sincerely want their party to win, and they can afford to help it with money. Others contribute because they have a personal interest in campaign issues. . . .

A unique field for democratic collectors is the restricted but lucrative circle of men and women who hold or want diplomatic appointments. An investigation of political contributions from these persons shows that an ambassadorship usually goes for about $50,000 on this odd job exchange. . . .

From the point of view of political ethics, there is nothing wrong about an American citizen contributing all he can to the party of his choice. . . . Contrary to the myth of "Wall Street power," rich men in America are neither numerous enough nor rich enough to exert a decisive influence on our democratic processes.

In fact, one of the weaknesses of the Republican party has been its reliance on rich men for monetary contributions. The record shows, for example, that from January 1 to February 29, 1952, the Republican National Committee received $143,687.77 in contributions over $100, and $5,070.42 in contributions less than $100. During a similar period, pledges to the Democratic National Committee ran $3,800.00 for contributions over $100, and $52,699.00 for contributions below $100.

These figures are important. They show that while the Republicans are receiving large sums from a few people, the Democrats go out and beat the bushes and bring back small pledges from a large number of people. Now a man who contributes a dollar or even a quarter to the Democrats feels he has a personal investment in that party. He will go out to vote for it, and most likely bring his wife and daughter. In the last instance, naturally, it is this vote which counts.

This fact, once it is understood by both parties, will serve more to limit individual contributions than any new legislation that might be put on the books.

Political contributions of another kind, however, are now coming under close scrutiny by Washington officials. Although banks and corporations have been scrupulously keeping to the letter of the law barring them from financial participation in campaigns, they have developed certain practices which can be interpreted as coming very close to the definition of "political activity." One of these is institutional advertising. For many years now, corporations have been in the habit of running "non-selling ads"—advertisements that do not feature any commodity or service. They simply sell an idea. It might be the very laudable idea of donating blood to the Red Cross, or accident-prevention. But some of the more recent advertisements, in which political implications have been seen, have been attacked as political campaigning.

It has now been revealed that Treasury agents are checking into the tax aspect of these ads—corporations might have claimed tax deductions on the grounds that the ads were legitimate business expenses. At the same time, it is understood that Justice Department lawyers are examining the matter in the light of the Smith-Connally Act prohibitions.

But if the Justice Department is as lenient with the advertisers as it has been with Big Labor activities in politics, corporations haven't much to worry about. Under the Smith-Connally and Federal Corrupt Practices Acts, labor unions are banned from making a contribution in connection with a Federal election. Yet during the 1944 campaign—just one year after the passage of the Smith-Connally Act—the CIO Political Action Committee alone spent $1,327,775.92 to elect Roosevelt. For this it was called on the carpet by the special committee investigating the presidential campaign. . . . The PAC admitted that it spent money to influence elections, printed pamphlets and generally made its weight felt. But, said the PAC, none of that money was given directly to a candidate, nor were the pamphlets approved by a candidate, and thus, smiled the PAC, it had not violated the letter of the law. The committee was not pleased with this explanation. It urged that "loopholes in the law which purportedly permitted this [political activity] be closed," and referred a test case to the Justice Department. At present (October 1952) the loopholes are still open and the Justice Department is still sitting on the test case.

Meanwhile, during the . . . [1948] campaign, the PAC and other labor groups were more active than before and reported spending $1,291,343, not including money collected and spent by local PAC and other labor groups, believed to have amounted to $5 million. . . .

Perhaps the best-behaved group among the Big Three has been Big Government—best-behaved according to the letter of the election laws. There have been relatively few outright violations of the Hatch Act by government officials, due perhaps to the

fact that Big Government does not have to infringe on the law
to get its political benefits. Dr. Goldman of Chicago University
puts it politely by saying: "The public treasury plays a large part
in the financing of party fortunes through economic decisions
favorable to party supporters and employment opportunities en-
hanced by the partisan affiliations of civil servants." . . .

As to political patronage, there are 2,518,000 men and women
now in Federal employ, representing about 5 per cent of the
estimated number of voters in this election. On the whole, they
have not been unduly influenced. There are few political buttons
on Washington lapels, no posters along the busy corridors of the
"temporary" government buildings. Moreover, civil servants who
have the misfortune of being Washingtonians still have no right
to vote. As to the rest of them, unless they show unusual indi-
viduality or temerity, they will probably vote for the party in
power, Hatch Act or no Hatch Act.

In . . . [the 1952] campaign, at least fifty cents out of every
dollar contributed to a candidate or party will go for radio and
television publicity. Another fifteen cents will pay for billboards,
posters, and snipe sheets. Mailed publicity will take another
eight cents, twelve cents will go for overhead, and ten cents of
the election dollar will be spent on trains and plane fares, field
workers and other miscellaneous expenses. . . .

During this [1952] campaign, it will cost a candidate $31,000
for an evening hour on all sixty-three stations taking NBC trans-
continental feeds. Should a candidate or party desire something
enjoyed by every major breakfast food company—fifteen minutes
a day on your living room screen during the four months preceding election day—he would have to pay $3,720,000 to one net-
work alone. Multiply that by three to include NBC, CBS, ABC
and the minor chains and independents, and you'll get the un-
believable total of $11 million. It will sound more believable if
you consider that the three networks got $2 million each from
the sponsors for just two weeks of convention coverage.

No candidate, naturally, can afford to pay such astronomic
prices in order to get his message across to the people. He may
turn to radio, but there again he will find that a 188-station coast-
to-coast hookup costs $25,814.50 an hour, or approximately $13,-

000 per minute for all networks. At such rates silence becomes truly golden, but a candidate cannot campaign in silence.

A group of congressmen and senators have seriously taken up the question of the cost of political radio and TV time. They argue that an honest candidate is not in business, and therefore should not be forced to bid for time on TV and radio in competition with such profitable enterprises as beer breweries and soap manufacturers.

But in analyzing the financial implications of this campaign, party planners will find that high-priced radio and TV time are not necessarily the key to electoral success. . . . A candidate appearing in person at a local railroad station has more vote-getting power than his flickering image reproduced electronically in the size of a flower vase. Also, he saves money that way. The White House wouldn't tell us how much President Truman's 272-speech tour cost him in 1948. But, armed with the information that he traveled 31,000 miles with a five-car train, we approached the railroads for an estimate and found that the whistle stops cost Truman about $30,000, including food, overnight parking, and sanitation charges. . . .

Both politicians and political scientists agree that this situation cannot continue. Party organizations spend half their time trying to collect money, and the other half shoveling it out for publicity, overhead, research, transportation, field workers' salaries, and other miscellaneous items. . . .

Several plans are now being considered to do something about election expenses. Senator Douglas is plugging a theory originally advanced by Theodore Roosevelt, that the government subvene the cost of political campaigns. This measure presents an obvious danger to our democratic processes. It is easy to see how unscrupulous government officials could use funds to favor friendly candidates and block the elections of their opponents.

Congressman Hale Boggs now heads a House Committee on Campaign Expenditures, and has imported a bright young lawyer from Louisiana to assemble a report on existing legislation with a view to its amendment and improvement.

Senator Hubert Humphrey feels strongest about the subject. He told us: "Existing [electoral] legislation is totally inadequate to assure clean and fair elections in the United States. Its limitations do not limit, its prohibitions do not prohibit. Loopholes in the various laws are so great that you could throw the White House through them, and follow it with the Washington Monument." The Senator wants immediate enactment of legislation "to provide penalties, and once and for all make sure that money cannot be used in undemocratic ways to influence American elections."

Our own study showed that following measures would help to bring campaign finances back to a sane and manageable level:

1. Institute the collection of party dues. At present, only the Communist and Socialist parties in the United States collect regular dues from their members. But there is no reason why Americans should not pay out a few dollars each year to relieve their major parties from continual financial worry.

2. Regulate campaign spending in primaries, which at present are not covered by law. In some states, particularly southern ones, a primary victory means automatic election, and the same rules should apply to them as apply in general elections.

3. Establish a permanent congressional committee charged with supervising and enforcing existing legislation as to maximum spending and contributions or activities by corporations, labor unions, and individuals.

4. Establish fixed and equitable rates for TV and radio time available to political candidates.

Some of these points are now being considerd by legislators and political scientists.

THE ELECTION

EDITOR'S INTRODUCTION

The first three articles in this section describe the mechanics and the history of the electoral college. The last of the three tells of efforts to abolish or to curtail the functions of this body, the objects of most proposals for electoral reform. A debate follows on the merits of direct popular election of the President, and the late Carl Becker offers a philosophic defense of the present electoral system. Although under certain circumstances the presidential election may, under our laws, be thrown into Congress, research for this volume turned up no argument for substituting congressional for popular election in some form.

Three principal proposals for electoral reform are under consideration by the present Congress. The so-called Lodge-Gossett Amendment, passed by the Senate in 1951 but pigeonholed in a House committee, would do away with the electoral college and substitute an electoral vote apportioned among presidential candidates in each state in ratio to their popular vote. Senator Smathers would combine that reform with a national presidential primary and provision for an interim election in case of the death or incapacity of the President. Representative Coudert of New York would retain the electoral college but would give it more representative character by having it elected in the same way as members of Congress—that is, two electors for each state chosen at large, as its senators are, and the others by congressional districts. Numerous views for and against these proposals are presented.

Other articles tell what happens if a President-elect dies and how the new ten-year limitation on presidential tenure works and discuss the merits of the constitutional amendment regulating presidential succession.

HOW WE ELECT A PRESIDENT [1]

On . . . the first Tuesday after the first Monday in November [every fourth year] the citizens of this nation . . . vote to elect the next President and Vice President of the United States. . . .

[1] From an article in *Journal of the National Education Association.* 41:424-5. October 1952. Reprinted by permission.

As provided by the Constitution of the United States, these elections have been held once every four years, beginning in 1789. No emergency has ever blotted out or postponed this fundamental privilege of the American people; in peace or war, in good times or bad, American citizens have selected a President every four years.

In setting up machinery for the selection of a President, the Constitution provided for electors from each state. Each state has as many electors as it has total number of representatives in the United States Senate and House of Representatives. All of these electors together are known as the electoral college. Today the electoral college has 531 votes. . . .

[At first] the system worked this way: Each state legislature had the power to choose the allotted number of electors for its state. The men thus chosen used their own judgment and elected our first President and Vice President: George Washington and John Adams.

Today the system works this way: As in 1788, each state has its allotted number of electoral votes. Since 1872 all state electors (except in two instances) have been chosen by popular vote. The actual machinery by which voters choose their electors varies from state to state. But the net result is this: The candidate who gets the most votes in a state is practically certain to get all the electoral votes of that state. Not since . . . [1948—see next article] have the electoral votes of a state split between two candidates.

On . . . the first Monday after the second Wednesday in December, the official electors of the states . . . meet in their respective state capitals to vote for our next President and Vice President. Constitutionally, these electors may vote for anyone whom they choose. Actually, each elector will already be pledged to a certain course of action. After the electors have voted, each state will certify the electoral ballots from the state and send the results to Congress to be counted. . . .

Because the electors are pledged to certain candidates, we ordinarily know the results of the election within a day or two after Election Day in November. But the election process, as set forth in the Constitution, is not complete till Congress has counted the votes.

If no presidential candidate receives a majority of electoral votes, the members of the House of Representatives—voting by states [with one vote for each state]—select the President from among the top three candidates. A candidate needs a majority —twenty-five or more votes—to be so elected.

If no vice-presidential candidate receives a majority of electoral votes, the members of the Senate—voting as individuals— select the Vice President from among the top two candidates. A candidate needs a majority—forty-nine or more votes—to be so elected.

ARE ELECTORS BOUND IN THEIR VOTES? [2]

The electoral college, to which the writers of the Constitution gave the right of independent choice, has become such an anachronism that only one passage in the recent Supreme Court opinions dealing with its independent character got any public attention. This was what was written in dissent by Justice Jackson for himself and Justice Douglas:

The whole electoral system at . . . best . . . is a mystifying and distorting factor in presidential elections which may resolve a popular defeat into an electoral victory [as in 1876 and 1888]. . . . At its worst it is open to local corruption and manipulation, once so flagrant [1876] as to threaten the stability of the country. To abolish it and substitute direct election of the President . . . would seem to me a gain for simplicity and integrity of our governmental processes.

For years a large body of public opinion has reflected this view, and recurrent efforts have been made in Congress to change the system. . . .

The comment by Justice Jackson may put new life in the effort, but so far it does not seem to have done more than to evoke the comment: "How true." Meanwhile, those chosen as the electors in each state—some directly, by having their names

    [2] From "The Supreme Court and the Electoral College," by Arthur Krock, chief of New York *Times* Washington bureau. New York *Times*. p 16. April 25, 1952. Reprinted by permission.

printed on the winning party ticket; some indirectly, because their national party ticket has carried the state—continue with rare exceptions to cast their ballots for the national candidates of their parties.

The exceptions have occurred when an elector has exercised the full right of independence granted him by the Constitution but denied to him by custom and party law. The Constitution simply says that each state legislature may determine "the manner" by which the electors shall be "appointed" and that they are to "meet in their respective states" and cast their ballots for President and Vice President, only one of whom, however, may be a resident of the same state as themselves. In 1948, though Tennessee gave a popular majority for President Truman and the regular Democratic ticket, one Democratic elector who had declined to promise to abide by such a result, as was his prerogative, exercised it further by casting his ballot for the candidates of the States' Rights Democrats.

This could not be and was not legally challenged. But the recent case before the Supreme Court turned on an Alabama law by which the legislature had lavishly delegated to the state political party committees the power to determine which citizens could vote and be candidates in the party primaries. Ben F. Ray, offering himself as a candidate for elector on the Democratic primary ticket, declined to sign a pledge exacted by the committee that if chosen, he would support "the nominees of the national convention of the Democratic party for President and Vice President. . . ." He argued that the constitutional grant of independence to electors was thereby illegally abridged.

The Alabama high court agreed with Mr. Ray. But the Supreme Court majority said the Constitution did not forbid the requirement of such a pledge by a political party from one who sought to run in its own primary. State law allowed him to run independently and unpledged if he chose: therefore, though chances were dim for the success of such an attempt in Alabama, this met the terms of the Constitution.

In that decision the majority tacitly approved the delegation of such large power to a party committee by a state legislature.

But the Alabama high court also had approved it, and positively. This suggests that a legislature might make the delegation to a single citizen. If so, the Supreme Court will have to take a second look at this decision.

HISTORY OF THE ELECTORAL SYSTEM [3]

What happens in November when the voters go to the polls? We are in the habit of saying the people vote for and elect a President, but that statement is not exactly accurate. No President of the United States has ever been elected directly by the people. Instead, the people vote for a slate of presidential electors who in turn select the President by their votes. In some states, as in the case in my own state of Iowa, the names of the electors do not appear on the ballot, but a vote for the candidate of any political party for President is held to be a vote for the elector nominated by the party from the district in which the vote is cast.

How and why did this system come about? The matter of the election of the President was one of the most hotly debated issues which arose in the Constitutional Convention of 1787. Election by direct vote of the people was proposed, but there were those who feared that the people would never be well enough informed about the candidates to vote intelligently. It must be remembered that communication was a slow and difficult process in those days, with no telephone, no radio, no television, no telegraph, and no daily newspapers available to everyone. Another argument against the direct election by the people was that it would give the large states too great an advantage.

Then a proposal, the so-called Virginia plan, to have the President elected by the Congress, was put forward. But this plan, it was pointed out, would mean that the head of one branch of the Federal Government would be chosen by another branch, thus violating the principle of separation of powers.

[3] From "Let Us Choose Our President on a More Equitable Basis in 1956," by Representative James I. Dolliver, (Republican, Iowa). *Vital Speeches of the Day.* 18:722-5. September 15, 1952. Reprinted by permission.

The next plan to be rejected was that the President should be elected by the governors of the states. Alexander Hamilton then proposed the selection of electors by the people, voting by districts in each state. A modification of the Hamilton suggestion would have had the electors appointed by the state legislatures.

The final plan as originally embodied in the Constitution was a compromise, reached only after lengthy discussion and several votes. It contained features or principles of each of the major plans suggested. It provided for the election of the President by electors appointed by each state "in such manner as the legislature thereof may direct." The electors, equal to the number of representatives and senators each state had in Congress, were to meet in their states and vote for two persons. The person having the highest number of votes, provided he also had a majority of the total number of electors, was to be President. The person having the next highest number of electoral votes was to be Vice President. In case no candidate had a majority, the House of Representatives was to choose the President, with each state, regardless of population, having but one vote. The Senate was to choose the Vice President under such circumstances, with each senator voting individually

Flaws in this electoral machinery soon became evident. It might be well to note here that while the Constitution of the United States represented a tremendous accomplishment and was one of the greatest documents produced by man in his attempt to govern himself, yet it was not perfect. As a matter of fact, the framers of the Constitution themselves realized this and carefully inserted a section providing a method of amending the Constitution. That this was a wise move is proved by the fact that we still have the Constitution as the basic document of our free society. We have not had any further constitutional conventions nor adopted any new constitutions. There has been no need for that. But twenty-two amendments have been adopted, and hundreds of others have been proposed and discussed. Two of the amendments—the twelfth in 1804 and the twentieth in 1933—corrected the provisions of the original Constitution which established the method of electing the President.

The discussion of the electoral college system in the Constitutional Convention clearly revealed that the electors were expected to be outstanding men in the respective states who would choose the President and Vice President from among the foremost men in the nation. But shortly after the adoption of the Constitution came one of the most significant developments in American history—the rise of political parties. As early as 1796 the influence of political parties made itself felt in the electoral system. John Adams, a Federalist, received the highest number of votes and was elected President. But the second highest number of votes went, not to Thomas Pinckney, who was the Federalist candidate for Vice President, but to Thomas Jefferson, the presidential candidate of the Republicans. We then had a situation where the President was of one political party and the Vice President of the opposition party.

In the next presidential election, that of 1800, further flaws appeared in the electoral college system. Thomas Jefferson was the presidential candidate of the Republicans and Aaron Burr was their vice-presidential candidate. Fearful of what had happened in the 1796 election, Burr insisted that he should be given an electoral vote comparable to that of Jefferson. The result was that Jefferson and Burr both received exactly the same number of electoral votes. The election was thrown into the House of Representatives, which at that time was controlled by the opposition party, the Federalists. After thirty-six ballots, Jefferson was finally chosen as President and Burr became Vice President.

The election of 1800 made it evident that some change would have to be made in the electoral system. Accordingly a constitutional amendment was proposed providing that each elector should vote separately for President and Vice President. The proposed amendment also contained provisions relative to the manner of counting the electoral vote and specified that the Vice President should have the same qualifications for office as the President. The twelfth amendment, after having been ratified by the required number of state legislatures, went into effect on September 25, 1804.

Even with the twelfth amendment, however, the electoral system proved to be something less than satisfactory. In the election of 1824, Andrew Jackson was defeated by John Quincy Adams in a contest decided in the House of Representatives. Jackson had a plurality of the popular vote cast. But we must remember at that time the electors in Vermont, New York, Delaware, South Carolina, Georgia, and Louisiana were chosen by the legislatures and no popular votes were recorded in those states.

The most significant thing about the election of 1824 was the scandal which arose from the charge that Henry Clay, who had received thirty-seven electoral votes for President, had been asked to swing his support to Adams in return for appointment as Secretary of State. There is virtually no historical evidence to support this charge. But it does illustrate that the situation was, as one writer has stated, "one which invited intrigue, and no doubt there was much bargaining and attempted trading of votes." The founding fathers established the electoral college as a device to avoid partisanship in the election of the President, but the election of 1824 made it very clear that the electoral college system could and had become the instrument of partisan politics.

There have been other alleged inequities as a result of the electoral college system. In 1876, Samuel J. Tilden, the Democratic candidate, received a majority of the popular vote, but numerous disputes arose during the counting of the electoral vote, involving in four instances the filing of double returns from the states. An electoral commission was created by Congress to rule on the disputed votes. By a series of 8 to 7 decisions it ruled against the Tilden electors, with the result that Rutherford B. Hayes was chosen President by a single electoral vote—185 to 184. Later, in 1888, Benjamin Harrison became President, even though Grover Cleveland had 100,000 more popular votes.

In spite of the imperfections which have been demonstrated in the electoral system over the years, only one further correction has been made since the twelfth amendment was adopted in 1804. The twentieth amendment to the Constitution, adopted in 1933, abolished the short lame-duck session of Congress and provided that the terms of senators and representatives should begin on January 3 and those of the President and Vice President on

January 20 of the appropriate years. This means that, should an election be thrown into the House of Representatives, in the case of the President, or into the Senate, in the case of the Vice President, the choice would be made by the members elected at the same time as the presidential election was held. Under the old system, the lame-duck Congress, which might have been of a different political complexion from that of the leading candidate, would have made the choice.

As noted earlier, the method of choosing the electors was left to the state legislatures. At the beginning, in most states, the legislatures themselves chose the electors. Popular election was soon substituted and became universal by 1860. It was not unusual during the early days of popular election for the state to employ the district system, under which one elector was chosen from each congressional district and two electors—corresponding to the two senators—were chosen at large. . . . Under the district system, the electoral vote was often divided among two or more candidates.

The competition of political parties brought the district system to an end in favor of a general ticket system under which a party could be credited with all the electors of a state simply by gaining a plurality of the popular vote in the state as a whole. It is this general ticket system which is in effect today. In other words, the political party receiving the greatest number of votes in a state gets the entire electoral vote of that state.

For all practical purposes, this means that those people who vote for the losing candidate in their state have no voice at all in the selection of the President, even though, in the nation as a whole, their candidate may receive more votes than any other. To put it bluntly, the minority in any state is disfranchised in a presidential election. There is no reason why the vote of one American should count for more than the vote of any other American, yet that is the situation under the present electoral system.

It also results in a lopsided vote in the electoral college, which fails to reflect the national sentiment. For instance, in the . . . presidential election in 1948, Harry Truman received 49.5 per cent of the popular vote, but he received 57 per cent of the electoral vote. Thomas Dewey, in the same election, received 45.1 per cent of the popular vote but only 35.6 per cent of the electoral vote. An even more extreme example is the presidential election of 1936, when Alf Landon received 36.5 per cent of the popular vote but only 1.5 per cent of the electoral vote, a discrepancy of 35 per cent.

Another serious objection to the present system is that it tends to overemphasize the vote in certain so-called pivotal states, especially those which have large electoral votes. Presidential candidates from doubtful states have a better chance of securing the nomination, since the party figures that a candidate will be able to carry his own state with its important bloc of electoral votes. The able man from the smaller state is almost automatically excluded from serious consideration.

Within the pivotal states, great attention is given to minority groups which may happen to be in a position to swing the balance of power to one side or the other. Time and again in presidential campaigns we see special attention being paid not to the voters of the nation as a whole, but to small minority groups within large states, groups which in numbers amount to only a tiny fraction of the voting population. The power of special interests is thus exaggerated and vastly overemphasized. Irresponsible control of political parties by small, organized minorities is invited. Small third party movements could throw all the electoral votes of a close state to whichever major party offered them the best deal. As I said during the debate on reform of the electoral college in the House on July 17, 1950, "always the battleground and the battle issues are planned to capture the larger states and to please the minorities who hold the balance of power in those states."

PLEA FOR DIRECT ELECTION [4]

"In proportion as agents to execute the will of the people are multiplied, there is danger of their wishes' being frustrated; some may be unfaithful, all are liable to err."

[4] From "Should the President Be Elected by Direct Popular Vote? Yes!" by John B. Andrews. *Forum.* 112:224-31. October 1949. Reprinted by permission.

In these words Andrew Jackson advanced the proposition that the law of presidential election was undemocratic and needed revision.

According to the Constitution of the United States, Article II, section I [see Appendix], special groups of electors in each state of the union were to elect the President of the United States. . . .

The first four presidential elections were conducted in accord with this original provision of the Constitution. In the election of 1789, when Washington was unanimously elected President, John Adams became Vice President. Behind-the-scenes wire pulling by Alexander Hamilton ensured that Adams should not rival Washington in votes, since there was no constitutional method of differentiating President from Vice President during the voting process.

The election of 1800 illustrated this difficulty more clearly, when Republican candidates Jefferson and Burr drew the same number of electoral votes. There was no doubt that the electors intended Jefferson for the presidency and Burr for the vice presidency, but the final vote had to be cast in the House according to law. Because of violent feeling against Jefferson, it took thirty-six ballots in the House to break the deadlock. (It was actually broken by Hamilton's personal influence.)

To clarify the voting the Twelfth Amendment [see Appendix] to the Constitution was adopted by the states before the 1804 election. This amendment provided for separate voting for President and Vice President, with a majority of the total number of ballots needed for election to either office. In the event that no candidate has a majority for the presidency, the House is to choose among the three highest candidates; a similar provision regarding the vice presidency gives the choice to the Senate

The electoral system developed by the Constitution framer and accepted ever since with very slight modification is undemocratic, cumbersome, anachronistic, unrealistic, and unrepresenta tive. When the Federal Convention met in 1787 in Philadelphia the form of the government to be established and the nature of its executive were still in doubt. On one premise the majorit agreed: all danger of monarchy was to be avoided and the presidency was not to be made too strong. It was obvious to these statesmen that the method of electing the President might have a far-reaching influence on his power in Federal affairs, and even within the states themselves. . . .

The Constitution framers were, of course, familiar with the danger of having the executive chosen by the legislature, but they also had experienced in their states the executive strength which rose from direct election of governors. In a choice between evils, the Convention leaned toward legislative election.

The formulation of the electoral system, originally outlined by Alexander Hamilton, at first pleased few but was finally adopted by the Constitutional Convention. Most of the gentlemen present agreed with Elbridge Gerry that "the popular mode of electing the Chief Magistrate would certainly be the worst of all."

History has given the lie to Mr. Gerry in illustrating the evils of the electoral system. The growth of two great political parties, the wide extension of the suffrage, and the picturesque national presidential campaigns have blinded us to the nature of the presidential election. The national election seems like direct election by the voters, and the electoral college seems like an old-fashioned formality. Still, as Professor William Anderson of the University of Minnesota points out:

> We must not forget that the legislature in any state can at any time legally provide a different way of choosing presidential electors, that it could even choose the electors itself or set up a special body of voters to choose them, that election by these electors is not the same as election directly by the voters . . . and that the electors are not legally bound to vote for the party candidate.

In any election, the electoral system denies representation to minorities within the various states. The party which gets the highest vote in each state elects its entire slate of presidential electors. Minorities get no representation because the electoral vote of each state cannot be split. Legally, the candidate who gets the largest number of electoral votes, not popular votes, is the winner.

Because of the electoral system, it is possible for the candidate winning the popular vote to fail of election. This has already happened three times in our history, and provides an extreme example of the undemocratic nature of our elective process. . . .

Because under the present system a President may be elected without having a popular majority, the present system is clearly undemocratic.

Because it protects an outmoded doctrine of state sovereignty, it is also unrepresentative. On a strict population basis, the small states are greatly overrepresented. Nevada, for example, has three electors for less than 100,000 population, while New York has 250,000 inhabitants to every elector it controls. The system does not justify itself by protecting the small states, because the twelve most populated states have more than half the electors. Nor are geographical sections protected, since the states of the Northeast (with Minnesota, Iowa, and Missouri as the western fringe of the region) have more than half the total vote.

The electoral college system and the consequent "key position" of certain large states has occasioned the doctrine of "availability" for choosing presidential candidates. Thus the ablest men may be and are by-passed while the man who can swing New York becomes a candidate. This is another indirect evil of our current system.

The electoral system, actually, reflects the states-rights doctrine which was branded anachronistic by the Civil War. In a loosely-knit federation of sovereign states, it was of course arguable that the President of the federation should be the choice of the state governments. Because this was the original concept, the electors met (and still meet) in the various state capitals, and the names of the electors are sent to the Secretary of State by the state governors. In case of a contested election in any state, it is settled by the state itself in accordance with state law.

Today, however, the President is not the representative of the various states; he is the chosen national leader of the people of the United States. In the course of our history, his position has become far stronger than was originally intended; and his relationship to the American people has become direct, instead of indirect. This relationship is reflected in the fact that Americans vote not for electors, but for presidential candidates; the electors themselves are unknown to most of the voters (some states even leave the names of the electors off the ballots).

The electoral system also reflects an anachronistic concept of the role of the American President. Originally, the Constitution framers tried to provide for a President as weak as would be consistent with orderly government. Executive power was feared, hated, and distrusted by the framers of the American Constitution. Largely for this reason they avoided direct contact between the President and the American electorate at large. Today, however, for better or for worse, we have the strongest Chief Executive in the democratic world. The American press, the radio, the movie and television screen ensure the President's intimate and direct contact with the American people. There is no valid reason for not recognizing this vital change.

In addition, the outmoded and undemocratic system outlined above is cumbersome, slow, and unwieldy. After the national elections in November (at which the actual decision is made), the electors meet on the first Monday after the second Wednesday in December to cast their rubber-stamp ballots for the President and Vice President. Once these are transmitted to Washington, they are published by the Secretary of State and copies are sent to the two Houses of Congress. On the sixth of January following, Congress meets in joint session to watch the counting of electoral ballots and take action on contested ballots, if any.

As a formality, the above procedure is expensive and time-consuming. So long as the electors merely rubber-stamp the November election, their role is meaningless. And if ever they should depart from the popular election results, their role would be autocratic.

The alternative constitutional method of presidential election, i.e., by the House of Representatives in case of tied electoral vote, is undemocratic on the face of it. A House election by states is on all counts unjust, and the possibility of allowing the members of Congress to make a President is an ever-present danger. Remember, in this connection, that one man (Alexander Hamilton) supposedly held in his hand the choice between Jefferson and Aaron Burr in the election of 1800! As Martin Van Buren declared in 1826: "There was no point on which the people of the United States were more perfectly united than upon the propriety, not to say indisputable necessity, of taking the election of President from the House of Representatives."

The ancient system of presidential election indirectly through the electoral college cries out for change; the direct, popular election of the President is a democratic necessity. Why has the old system remained so long? Partly because change is resisted by the very terms of the Constitution governing amendment; partly because many Americans are unaware of the existence of the indirect system; partly because we are suffering from an inaccurate understanding of the nature of our Federal Government.

The pre-1860 concept of the United States as a union of sovereign states exists no longer; the sovereign states, by the same token, have been discarded. The exigencies of history have forced this country into a strong centralized form of government, headed by a strong executive with very direct control over the people of the United States. Since this is true of the government and of its executive, it is equally true that the people of the United States must establish a strong and very direct control over their President. His direct election by all the people clearly furthers this end.

AGAINST DIRECT ELECTION [5]

When we as a state are now a member of a slowly evolving United Nations, we can learn much by comparing the growth of the United Nations with the formulation of our own Federal Union. We do not want to see a world state in which each man has one vote, because we would be outvoted by China, Russia, and India, three nations with ideas of government quite different from our own.

When the United States became a nation, Rhode Island did not trust New York or Pennsylvania. Therefore, it, like all the

[5] From "Should the President Be Elected by Direct Popular Vote? No!" by Thomas J. Brown. *Forum.* 112:224-31. October 1949. Reprinted by permission.

other states, entered a compact, our Constitution, which reserved many rights to the states.

Among the rights which the small states were granted was overrepresentation in the Senate and in the electoral college on a strict population basis. If, in the Federal Constitution, we gave excess representation to Rhode Island, it was because Rhode Island feared the power of its larger neighbors. If today Rhode Island indirectly takes advantage of the fact that it once feared New York by continuing to have two senators while New York has only two, this is not too great a price to pay for the advantages that have accrued to the Union as a whole.

In fact, we have profited much more from our federal system than we have lost by its occasional anomalies, and the question before us is whether or not we would gain by doing away with a specific part of our federal system, the electoral college, and by substituting for it the direct election of the President by popular vote. . . .

Although the federal form of government has its weaknesses, it has its strengths as well. Functions reserved to the forty-eight states and prohibited to the Federal Government prevent the central government from becoming unbearably top-heavy and inefficient. The dwindling but still important power of the states serves to protect the citizens from the assumption of dictatorial power by a Washington administration.

Today we want the United States to have the final authority when we dispose of Marshall Plan aid to Europe. We do not want any or all of the nations of Europe to be able to decide how much of our income shall go to aiding Europe. We do not even want them to be able to decide what percentage of the whole shall be given to any specific nation. We do expect them to consult with each other and with us. This is obviously a looser type federation taking form. And, in the larger federation it is perhaps easier to see the importance of maintaining the functions and independence of local units.

We certainly should not forget that the United States is not only a government composed of states. It is also composed of important widely varying sections. The electoral college and our federal form helps protect each of them from domination by other sections. Today, for instance, the southern states would lose most of their remaining influence if a nation-wide majority were required for voting. . . .

When the Constitution was adopted, we did not have universal suffrage. Parties were ill-defined. Washington, when he was elected, was not a party candidate. Jefferson, the leader of the Republicans, and Hamilton, the leader of the Whigs, both were members of his cabinet. Nevertheless it was assumed that the electoral college would, in fact, be better qualified to elect the President than the voters would be. This was the product of the fear of power. These men feared "tyranny." They knew that the worst tyranny might well be "the tyranny of the majority." They were concerned with the protection of minorities. After all, the Bill of Rights is a protection for the ultimate minority of one.

The world they lived in was simpler than the world we live in. Each individual was of more importance to them. They did not see that one day one group of men might look to the government for aid against another group. But the restrictions they put upon the government to prevent the "tyranny" which they feared have worked well and are, it seems to me, our best protection against a different form of tyranny today.

To turn to our present problems, we have universal suffrage but we face problems which universal suffrage is not competent to solve. Recently the British devalued the pound drastically and dramatically. It is safe to say that most people both here and in Britain have no clear idea of what the ultimate effect of this action may be. It is also safe to say that the action was forced upon the British Government by a friendly and well-intentioned American Government. It is certainly possible to believe that the British Government was right. But it is hard to see what value a general election in either country would have had upon the matter before the British Government either accepted or rejected the position of the Government of the United States. Afterwards, if the results are bad enough to either or both countries, the electorate certainly can and will turn out the government whose policies have failed. . . .

All governments, "tyrannies" and "democracies" included, want to stay in power. But within all countries there are "factions" or "parties" opposed to the party in power. The basic concept on which we work is a concept of responsibility. The party in power is answerable to the people at every election. To be answerable there must be an effective opposition. Anything which tends to perpetuate the tenure of the party in power weakens our form of government.

It is my contention that widespread suffrage by itself tends in this direction. The election of the President by direct popular vote would increase the tendency because of the great advantage which our mass media of communication give to any man in office. Obviously we should strengthen our universal suffrage, not by giving the voters the relatively artificial choice between two men, but by the much more important choice of electors. The electors, not pledged to a party candidate, could choose the best man regardless of party. . . .

Direct popular election of the President . . . would necessitate a uniform national suffrage and election law as well. If the President is to be the direct representative of "all the American people," then the franchise must extend to all uniformly, regardless of their state of residence. Now it cannot be denied that varying state laws with regard to suffrage are inconvenient and, in many cases, downright undemocratic. During the war years, many intelligent Americans were disfranchised because war conditions forced them to move from state to state. In any and every year, most of the southern states manage to disfranchise their Negro population by means of the poll tax, the literacy tests, and other evasions. According to the Constitution of the United States, the source of the right to vote and of rules governing the suffrage rests with the states, subject to certain qualifications in the Federal Constitution. The states are in general to fix the "times, place and manner of holding elections," as well.

Again, the arrangements concerning the suffrage and election are basic to our federal form of government, and to insist on changing them out of hand involves a basic misunderstanding of federalism. If we are to substitute centralized government for the federal system, let us do so after due deliberation of its merits and demerits. Let us not slide into centralization without understanding its significance.

An equally strong objection to the direct election of the American President is that this step would further increase the broad powers of our Chief Executive. It is obvious that the present power assumed by our President is far stronger than originally granted him in the Constitution. Recurring wars and emergencies have slowly but definitely added to presidential power, until today our Chief Executive is the strongest democratic leader in the world. Once very carefully defined, the concept of "emergency government" and "emergency powers" has been enlarged since 1933 so that the President now feels qualified to declare an "emergency" at his own discretion, and to assume such powers as the right to enjoin strikes and settle labor disputes.

Those who advocate direct election of the President openly support a further increase in his authority. What the benefits of such an increase are to be, we are not told. Nor are we enlightened as to the proposed checks on executive authority to prevent the rise of dictatorship. Such checks are obviously imperative. . . .

Today we have not only the growth of the power of the President, but the growth of the power of the presidency. The man has become an institution. There are almost two million Federal employees. Most of them, protected by Civil Service, or appointed without this protection, think of themselves as part of the administration. Washington made 65 Federal appointments; President Truman thus far has made 1,800.

It has been argued that the indirect electoral system may cause the election of a President not of the majority's choosing. . . .

In truth, and in fact, the history of our presidential elections proves the converse. . . . In only two instances in our history (and both times the popular vote was very close), did the electoral vote go against the wishes of the majority. The danger of a President's election by a minority is therefore very remote. It exists, of course, and its existence serves to remind potential demagogues that more than popular support is necessary to win a national election in this country. Small but independent states, minority but vital regions—both must give at least part of their support to the successful presidential candidate. Such minority representation is in fact an integral part of our successful federal system.

One further objection to the direct election of the President is the increase in Federal expenditures which such a change would entail. The Federal Government, as we pointed out above, would be responsible for uniform suffrage laws, uniform election procedure, and for the management and operation of the polls themselves. The simple enforcement of universal suffrage in itself would add tremendously to the Federal burden (if such a principle could be enforced at all). The Federal failure to enforce universal suffrage would, of course, be an even more dismal failure than that of the states, and one that would add propaganda material to our enemies' dockets.

THE WILL OF THE PEOPLE [6]

No doubt, there is something to be said against the electoral system. There is, however, something to be said for it. The essential and relevant thing to be said about it, whether for or against, is that it is a fundamental factor in guaranteeing our "two-party" system, and that it makes it difficult if not impossible today for any major party to be organized on purely class or sectional lines. This may be a good thing or a bad thing. But in either case it is worth while to examine the electoral system, not in the light of what might conceivably happen in a non-existent presidential election, but in the light of what has actually happened in past elections, and what is likely to happen in elections in the immediate future. . . .

Beginning with the election of Jackson in 1828 [the 1824 election was thrown into the House of Representatives], there have been thirty presidential elections. In all of these the successful candidate received a majority of the electoral votes, so that in

[6] From an article by Carl Becker, late professor emeritus of history, Cornell University. *Yale Review*. 34, no3:385-404. Spring [March] 1945. Reprinted by permission.

no case has the election devolved on the House of Representatives. In nineteen of the thirty elections the successful candidate received a majority of the total popular votes cast. In nine of the remaining eleven elections the successful candidate, although not receiving a majority of the total popular votes cast, received a plurality—more of the popular votes than his chief rival. In only two elections out of the thirty did the successful candidate receive less of the popular votes than the defeated candidate. These two elections were those of 1876, in which Hayes (elected) received 47.95 percent, and Tilden (defeated) received 50.94 per cent; and the election of 1888, in which Harrison (elected) received 47.82 per cent, and Cleveland (defeated) received 48.66 per cent.

From this survey of what has happened it is clear that if in all thirty elections the decision had been determined by majority of the electoral votes, we would have had the same Presidents we have had, except that Tilden instead of Hayes would have been President in 1876, and Cleveland instead of Harrison in 1888. In short, the electoral system has defeated the popular will, in so far as the popular will can be expressed by a majority or plurality vote, only twice in one hundred and sixteen years. And maybe, after all, only once. It is still uncertain whether Tilden was defeated by the electoral system or by skulduggery in counting the votes. In view of all this, I think we can say with confidence that the people of the United States do elect their President.

I think, indeed, that we can go further, and say that the "will of the people" is more likely to prevail under the present system of registering the popular pluralities by states than it would be if the elections were decided by a plurality of the popular votes in the country as a whole. But this raises another question altogether, and a very difficult one to answer. What, after all, is "the will of the people," and how can it be most adequately expressed?

The will of the people is at best an intangible thing, and it is a delusion to suppose that it can be determined in all circumstances by majority vote. Majority vote was accepted by the founding fathers for want of something better—a practical device which, as Jefferson said, was the only alternative to "force, which ends inevitably in military despotism." But majority vote, counting heads, expresses the will of the people well enough only so long as the heads are all much alike, only so long as the minority is willing to accept the decision of the majority and let it go at that. Generally speaking, the minority will accept the decision of the majority without breaking heads so long as it feels that nothing vital is at stake, and that there is another day coming when the minority will itself become the majority and get its own back. But if the minority feels that it has no such chance, that its minority status is permanent, and that the interests of the ruling majority are irreconcilable with its own, then majority vote no longer expresses the will of the people: it expresses the will of a part of the people only, and results in the unwilling subjection of the minority to the imposed will of the majority.

Only once in the history of the United States (I am thinking now of minorities, not in terms of racial groups which through certain forms of discrimination have a permanent minority status, but in terms of the major political parties) has this situation existed—in the sectional conflict over slavery that ended in disunion and civil war. Apart from the slavery issue, no fundamental difference of interest has arisen to disturb the democratic device of majority vote as a method of determining the will of the people. . . .

And in fact, in no presidential election, apart from that of 1860, has anything of profoundly serious import occurred. The reason is that a presidential election is normally a contest between two major political parties which, in respect to the principles they profess and the measures they advocate, do not differ in any matter of fundamental importance. The contest turns on issues so far from that that both parties can with good conscience appeal to the same classes for their suffrage, and either party can safely be regarded, in case it wins the election, as representing the will of the people in respect to all fundamental rights and interests. . . .

There are, no doubt, many reasons for this situation, but one of them is the electoral system of registering the results of the popular vote by states. This system makes it impossible for any political party to win a national election, even though it has a majority of the popular votes cast, unless the votes it polls are properly distributed throughout the country; and no party has much chance of getting such a distribution if it represents exclusively the interests of any section or class. It can get the necessary strategic distribution of the popular vote only if it is willing to appeal to the interests of many sections and to the interests of all classes—agriculture and industry, capital and labor, rich and poor, progressives and conservatives—in a sufficient number of states to win a majority of the electoral votes. . . .

Thus the system of federated governments, and the close connection between state and Federal elections, works hand in hand with the electoral system to prevent any party from being a major party capable of winning a national election unless it is willing to pay the price. The price is that it must be all things to all sections, tempering its policy to the predominant interests, and trimming its sails to the prevailing winds of sentiment, in virtually all of the states in the Union. . . .

In these various ways, and through these intricate procedures, the people of the United States do now elect their President. But all systems change, and this one is not immune from change. There is already some agitation in favor of separating state and national elections. If this were done it might mitigate one of the defects of the system by giving the voters clear-cut issues. There are also certain "political action" groups, and others are in the process of organization, which are having some effect on the method of election. Some of these are pressure groups, some of them are disinterested. But it is difficult to see how any or all of these can change the fundamental conditions that determine the nature of the two major political parties; or do more than provide the party leaders with a greater number of special vote-getting groups to take into account.

If there is to be any radical modification of the present system, it is most likely to come as a result of the intensification of what is called the "class struggle." In many industrialized countries, the laboring classes, under pressure of the class struggle, have become political parties representing class interests. This may happen here, although it would be more difficult for it to happen. But if the country, as it becomes more highly industrialized throughout, becomes again a house "divided against itself," not on sectional but on class lines, so that the conflict between the privileged and the underprivileged is nation-wide and takes precedence over all other interests; and if this conflict should be sufficiently prolonged—in such a situation the result would undoubtedly be a gradual reorganization of major parties along economic class lines in both state and national politics. In that case, politics would be more than a game played for low stakes; our elections would be embittered to the danger point; and it would be no longer easy to take the result of a close election with the same good-humored resignation that we now exhibit. But it has not yet come to that, and I for one should be sorry to see it come to that.

Meanwhile, the merits of the system as it now works far outweigh its defects. Its supreme merit, for a country so large and diversified in its interests and prejudices and points of view as ours, is that all of its pressures and restraints tend to keep the nation politically united and politically stable. It requires the political leaders, whether in or out of office, to go slow, keep pretty close to the center, and to cultivate at all times the high political art of conciliation and compromise—the art of soft-pedaling the issues that threaten to divide the people and holding fast to the issues on which they can remain united.

It is surely one of the fine ironies of history that the electoral system, devised by the founding fathers to nullify the will of the people in choosing a President, has in fact turned out to be one of the devices which enable the will of the people to prevail.

LODGE ARGUES FOR HIS PLAN [7]

The present indirect system of electing the President and Vice President of the United States is neither fair, honest, accurate, certain, nor democratic. At fault is the so-called electoral college. It should be abolished.

In its place should be established a system in which the electoral vote for the President and Vice President is counted in

[7] From "Should the United States Abolish the Electoral College? Yes!" by Henry Cabot Lodge, Jr., then a Republican Senator from Massachusetts, now chief United States delegate to the United Nations. *Rotarian.* 75:25+. July 1949. Reprinted by permission.

proportion to the popular vote. A joint resolution proposing such a system has been introduced in the 81st Congress: I am one of eleven senators, sponsoring it in the upper house. [Senate Joint Resolution 2, 81st Congress, 1st session.]

The electoral system we now have is based on the eighteenth-century idea that each of the states would name its outstanding citizens to join with similar leading citizens from other states in selecting the President. The people were not trusted to choose their own President—hence it was to be done for them by the "electoral college." Actually, it has never worked that way. The electors soon became automatons, exercising no discretion at all, and a whole set of defects came into existence which had been neither foreseen nor approved by the framers of the Constitution. Here are some of those defects.

First is the "unit rule" which credits the winner in every state with all the votes, including those which were cast against him. In the 1948 elections 6 million votes were cast in New York State. Governor Dewey ran only 60,000 votes ahead of President Truman in that state, but that gave him all New York's 47 electoral votes. In the nation Governor Dewey polled nearly half of the 46 million popular votes. Yet he received only 189 out of the 531 electoral votes. The unit rule makes a campaign in any state a gamble; it is an all-or-nothing proposition.

A second defect in the present system is that it makes possible a situation in which the candidate with the most popular votes receives the least electoral votes. This has actually happened three times.

In 1824 Andrew Jackson secured a popular plurality of 50,000 votes over John Quincy Adams but failed of the presidency when the election was decided by the House of Representatives. In 1876 Hayes became President by the majority of one electoral vote, even though Tilden actually received 258,000 more popular votes then he did. In 1888 Cleveland lost the presidency, even though he had a popular vote of 5,540,054 against Harrison's 5,444,337.

The passions which bitter elective struggles engender could well lead to violent and bloody conditions—as almost proved to be the case in 1876. Had Samuel J. Tilden taken a belligerent attitude, the nation might well have been plunged into civil strife. Fortunately he refused to listen to the pleas of his followers to seize the presidency by force.

A third defect is the method provided for breaking deadlocks—which result when no candidate obtains a majority of the electoral votes. (In United States politics a candidate has a majority when he has more votes than his opponent in a two-man race, or more votes than all his opponents together have in a contest with three or more entrants. He has a plurality when he has more votes than any other candidate.) The Constitution provides that in such a case the election of the President shall be cast into the House of Representatives, where he shall be elected by a majority vote of the members—not voting as individual members, however, but voting by states with one vote to a state. It is, therefore, possible for twenty-five small states, with a total membership of only 89 out of a total of 435 members, to control the election.

Still fresh in our minds is the feeling of frustration we experienced on election night last November [1948] when it seemed possible that we would enter the year without an elected President. That would have been an actuality had Governor Dewey carried any two of the states of California, Illinois, or Ohio. With all three of these close-vote states, he would have won; with any two of them he would have deprived President Truman of a majority; that is, his votes and those of Governor Thurmond, who was also in the three-man race, would have totaled more together than Truman's. Thus the election would have gone into the House. A deadlock there could quite conceivably have found the nation without a President at noon on inauguration day—with a rush to the statute books to see what, if anything, the law says about succession in such preposterous cases.

A fourth defect is the uselessness of the electors. They exercise no independent judgment. They are mere rubber stamps—and inaccurate rubber stamps at that. The people know the candidates for President annd Vice President; rarely do they know the identity of the electors for whom they actually vote. Such "go-betweens" are like the appendix in the human body. While it does no good and ordinarily causes no trouble, it continually exposes the body to the danger of political peritonitis.

Moreover, it is possible for a dangerous situation to arise in a close election where one or two electoral votes may have a decisive effect. The danger lies not so much in the possibility that the delegate might forget his pledge—though a Tennessean showed us last November how an elector can vote for anybody he pleases, regardless of the popular vote. It lies more in the possibility that he might be sick, or insane, or suddenly killed. These risks are unavoidable for individual human beings; it is not necessary, however, to inject them into our system for electing a President.

There are numerous other defects in the electoral college system. There is the encouragement it gives to fraud, posing strong temptations for the boss and the machine in a pivotal state where just a few more votes will tip the entire electoral balance in favor of their man. Also, there is the theoretical possibility that the electors would abuse their power and disregard the Constitution. Those who set up dictatorships are often careful to preserve constitutional forms. This form serves no good purpose. Still another defect revealed itself last November when (in Alabama) the obsolete and preposterous electoral college machinery was legally maneuvered so as to prevent the voters from casting their ballots for a duly nominated candidate of a political party. I need go no further. The lessons of 1948, as of 150 years before, impress upon us all the great need for reform.

The kind of reform I favor is that embodied in Senate Joint Resolution 2. It proposes an amendment to the Constitution abolishing the electoral college and establishing a system of electing the President and Vice President by the people of the several states. The electoral vote of each state would, however, be retained—but only as an automatic counting device. As at present, each state would be entitled to a number of electoral votes equal to the whole number of senators and representatives to which such state may be entitled in the Congress. Each candidate would be credited with exactly the same proportion of the electoral votes as he received of popular votes.

The person having the greatest number of electoral votes for President would be President. If two or more persons should have an equal and the highest number of votes, the one for whom the greatest number of popular votes were cast would be the President. The Vice President would likewise be elected.

Under such a system the United States citizen would at last have a legal voice in his choice of President—not a mere expression of preference as at present. His vote would count for the man he intended to support and never, as now often happens, for the man he opposed. Furthermore, the electoral vote, worked out to the third decimal place if necessary, would exactly reflect the popular vote.

Some ask what would have happened in the immediate past campaign if this plan had been law. It is easy to apply the amendment retroactively, of course, but I cannot emphasize too strongly that, had the measure been in effect, citizens would not have voted as they did. The whole composition of the popular vote would have been different. Supposing, however, that they had voted exactly as they did, this would have been the result: Truman, 258 electoral votes; Dewey, 221.4 electoral votes. The actual result was Truman, 303 electoral votes; Dewey, 189 electoral votes.

A question often asked about this proposal is: "Wouldn't it encourage the formation of many little parties and thus weaken the two-party system?" It would not. The proponents of the resolution are strong believers in the two-party system and oppose anything which would threaten us with a multiplicity of parties. Indeed, this amendment should greatly reduce the present weight of splinter parties and special pressure groups, for it deprives them of the bargaining power they now possess by virtue of their ability so often to swing all the electoral votes of key states to one or the other major candidate—as witness the 1948 elections in New York.

Furthermore, this reform would definitely encourage the two-party system in the so-called one-party sections of the country.

With the exception of the President and Vice President, we elect all our public officials by popular vote. If there has been no proliferation of splinter parties within the states for local, state and Federal officers under a direct, popular vote system, there seems little likelihood that they would flourish on a national scale.

The argument is also made that the proposed amendment would impinge upon state political power. The reply, again, is that it would not. It in no way meddles with state sovereignty or the rights of any state to specify the qualifications of its voters or the manner in which they shall vote or have their votes counted. We leave the purity of the ballot box entirely within state control.

Some, too, have questioned the provision that the person winning a plurality of electoral votes, rather than a majority as at present, would be President. Election by plurality is the general rule in the United States; we elect local and state officials and senators and congressmen by plurality. Indeed, in actuality we elect the President on a plurality basis, for a plurality of people in any given state decide which candidate shall receive all that state's electoral votes. In terms of popular vote, about half our Presidents have been plurality—but not majority— choices. President Truman is one; he received more popular votes than either of his two opponents, but less than the two together.

Some, too, claim that the proposal does not go far enough— that we should scrap not only the electoral college but the electoral vote as well and elect our President and Vice President by nation-wide popular vote.

To do so would be to make national campaigns a matter of complete national control; it would obliterate state lines altogether in presidential elections. The state of Georgia, for example has an eighteen-year voting age. To be on a parity with Georgia, all states would have to reduce their voting age to eighteen years under an absolute, direct, popular vote.

Again, under such a system, sectionalism would be aggravated. In a sectional controversy it would be a contest of gathering up the greatest volume of votes in one area to outvote some other area.

Finally, there are those who say that because the electoral college has been a part of the Constitution ever since its original adoption we should be most reluctant to abolish it. The answer to that is in the history books.

By adopting this reform now we will avoid the political crisis which is certain to come, sooner or later, if we continue to rely on our present defective and obsolete electoral system.

PATMAN OPPOSES LODGE PLAN [8]

The democratic system of electing a President and Vice President of the United States has worked out well for 160 years. Any fundamental change in it should be weighed in all its implications.

It is true that the electoral college has been changed by custom, practice, and law to an entirely different instrument from that conceived by the fathers of the Constitution. Yet, though haphazardly evolved, it has functioned successfully to represent the opinion of the country as a whole. Only three times have there been elections in which the candidate chosen for President by electoral vote was not the man who received the majority, or at least a plurality, of the popular vote. The exceptional circumstances in those cases deprive them of any significance in considering the electoral college system.

In the election of John Quincy Adams (1824) two electors voted contrary to the will of the people, and the election was decided by the House of Representatives. Each state legislature can, if it wishes, prevent the recurrence of such a case by passing a law requiring each elector to vote as directed by the plurality vote of the people in the district which he is elected to represent.

In the case of Hayes' election over Tilden (1876), who had the popular majority, the question was one of an incorrect tally of the votes, which had been partly remedied by act of Congress. Polk (1845), Taylor (1849), Lincoln (1861), and

[8] From "Should the United States Abolish the Electoral College? No!" by Wright Patman, then a Democratic Representative from Texas. *Rotarian.* 75:25+. July 1949. Reprinted by permission.

Wilson (1913), who became President in those years, each carried only a small plurality of the popular vote. However, they probably represented as great a proportion of the electorate as could be enlisted by any one candidate in their times.

The present system, whereby the candidate receiving a plurality of the popular vote in a state is credited with all that state's electoral votes, has worked to maintain a very desirable balance of power between the more populous states and the rest of the states. Our entire system of representative government from its inception has recognized minority influences as well as numerical superiority. The United States House of Representatives, for example, may not represent at any one time the aggregate wishes of all the people, since each congressman is elected by varying majorities in his own district.

Some modernization in the operation of our electoral college is desirable. In these days of instant communication there should be no lag of several months between the casting of the popular vote and the meeting of the electoral college. Perhaps the actual meeting of the electors could be eliminated. These formalities may be archaic; the system itself is not.

On first examination the Gossett-Lodge amendment seems an admirable step toward modernization of our Constitution. Further study, however, reveals in it several dangerous and far-reaching implications. One is this: Because the proposed system would credit each person for whom votes were cast for President in each state "with such proportion of the electoral votes thereof as he received of the total vote," the plan would greatly stimulate and encourage the formation, merger, and development of minority parties. Our present two-party system would be destroyed.

Let me ask this: Why is it that neither the extreme right—the Fascist groups—nor the extreme left—the Communist group—has offered any objection to this amendment? Can it be that they see it as an opening through which they can slip into our government and undermine its democratic nature? For the first time these radical groups could obtain electoral votes for their candidates for President and Vice President.

We have had 105 splinter parties in the United States in the last 160 years. Seventy-three of those parties have elected one or more members to Congress or nominated a presidential candidate, but none has ever garnered enough votes to elect a President. The two-party system, which I believe the strongest kind of representative government, has prevailed.

Yet, under this proposed amendment, we could expect to see the rise of many new parties—the Communist, the Dixiecrat, the Ku Klux Klan; parties representing the North, East and West; parties representing the farmers, the manufacturers, the laborers; parties representing racial and religious minorities. In themselves, minority parties are not a menace. Our government has flourished despite the sporadic existence of the 105 splinter parties I have mentioned.

But here is the example of a democracy struggling with a multiplicity of parties: France has nine principal parties, each of which has one or more affiliated parties. An integrated program cannot be developed by a government composed of so many diverse elements. Its leadership is tossed back and forth between a succession of premiers, none of whom can unite the government.

Under the Gossett-Lodge proposal the voting for President is no longer by states, but by the country as a whole. Under the existing system the states have the right to determine the qualifications of their electors and the placing of names on the ballot. Thus the proposed system would encourage minority candidates to turn to the Federal courts for protection of their rights, for a place upon the ballot, and for a share of the electoral vote. Federal supervision could easily follow a few court decisions favorable to minority parties.

The most popular argument for the amendment is that it will reduce the possibility of a candidate winning the election with a minority of the popular vote. I believe the converse to be true. Let us explore the idea. Because of traditional voting restrictions in the eleven states of the "Solid South," an electoral vote in that section represents only about 40,000 votes. In the other thirty-seven states an electoral vote represents more than 110,000 popular votes. It would be a bad swap for the Republicans to trade large blocks of electoral votes in states they usually carry for the very few electoral votes they would gain in the South under this proposed plan. The Republicans could well be voting themselves out of existence by approving this amendment. . . .

Supporters of the new plan also contend that it would eliminate the "lost" popular votes—the ones cast for the losing candidate in each state. Let us look at that argument, too. Small states, like Delaware, with only three electoral votes, would find this to be the case: With their few votes divided among two or more candidates, they would be giving the successful candidate a lead of only one half, one quarter, one eighth or one sixteenth of the electoral vote. No, the "lost" votes would, I believe, merely be transferred from the state to the national level.

Finally, let us consider the provision of this amendment covering the case in which two candidates might receive an equal number of electoral votes. It is proposed that in such a case the candidate having the greatest number of popular votes would be President. No matter how small his plurality—no matter how the vote was split among many candidates—he would direct the course of our government. The House of Representatives would be completely by-passed in a close or tie race.

To sum up, then. I oppose this proposed change because it would:

1. Encourage a multiplicity of parties and destroy our two-party system.

2. Encourage minority parties represented only by electoral votes to campaign for legislative representation.

3. Open the way for Federal supervision of state elections.

4. Increase the possibility of a candidate winning an electoral majority despite a popular minority.

5. Increase the possibility, in the case of a tie vote, that the President would represent the choice of a minority.

LODGE'S PROPOSALS WEIGHED [9]

The choice of Presidents has been criticized sharply ever since the republic's early days. Senator Lodge (Republican,

[9] From "The Lodge-Gossett Plan," by Herbert Wechsler, professor, Columbia University Law School. *Fortune*. 39:138-46. June 1949. Reprinted from the June 1949 issue of *Fortune* by special permission of the editors. Copyright 1949, Time, Inc.

Massachusetts) and Congressman Gossett (Democrat, Texas) have revived the attack. . . . As with many reforms, the Lodge-Gossett resolution involves gains and losses to be balanced.

The proposals would change the complicated constitutional pattern in four particulars:

(1) The electors would be abrogated as a human agency, while preserving each state's electoral votes numbered by its total representation in Congress as the measure of its influence on the election. Nevada's 110,000 would still count three, New York's 13,500,000 only forty-seven.

(2) The right to vote, now granted by the states alone, would be safeguarded by the Federal Constitution.

(3) Where each state now is free to say how its electors shall be chosen—and thus fix the rule that measures distribution of its electoral votes—a single novel standard would be substituted: a state's electoral votes would be apportioned among all candidates on the ballot in proportion to their votes within the state. Instead of speaking to the country with a single voice regardless of differences among its voters, a state would mirror the division in the allocation of its electoral votes.

(4) Both the requirement of a majority of electoral votes and the provision for congressional selection where no candidate attains it would be abrogated. The candidate with the most electoral votes would be elected, and in a tie the decision would depend upon the popular vote.

It would be difficult to take a brief in defense of the electors, unnecessary as automata, unacceptable as independent agencies of choice; they ought to go. Nor is there longer room for difference of opinion as to Federal protection of the right to vote; it should be fixed securely in the Constitution. And undoubtedly these two changes would have been adopted long ago but for the fact that they are usually coupled with more controversial changes. Such is the case again with the Lodge-Gossett proposal.

The controversial issues lie in the proposals to require proportional division of each state's electoral votes, to make an electoral plurality suffice for election, and to eliminate choice by the

House of Representatives. These would work a major alteration in our presidential politics.

Under prevailing practice, no importance is attributed to the extent of a successful candidate's advantage in a state he carries; he wins its electoral votes completely by a small plurality and gets no more if he sweeps the state. By the same token, state minorities have no political expression; they must prevail, or their votes are washed out. Neither the 2,987,647 New York voters who supported Dewey against Roosevelt nor the 2,781,590 who preferred Truman to Dewey had the slightest influence. There is in total consequence a real chance that any election may select a President who lacks a popular plurality throughout the country. . . .

There are other no less impressive dangers. Since small margins of difference may determine large and possibly decisive groups of electoral votes, any voting block that may appear to hold the balance of decision in important doubtful states is granted disproportionate political importance. This is to some extent intrinsic to all popular elections; a close division must give some groups a decisive voice, involving influence that far transcends numbers. The limit is that no group demand concessions that outrun the tolerance of other necessary elements of a plurality. Yielding to Wallace and the Communists in 1948 would have cost either major candidate far more votes than he could have hoped to gain. But even within this important limit, casting state electoral votes as units tends to give organized minorities enormous influence in strategic states.

The possibilities of exploitation by such groups within a state are small, however, as compared to those presented to a voting block with sufficient concentration to gain state pluralities and thus win electoral votes. In any close election such a movement may imperil popular selection by preventing either major candidate from winning an electoral majority, thus casting the choice on the House voting by states. In such a case the twenty-five least populated states—with little more than one sixth of the citizenry—could theoretically join to elect a President.

In practice there is small chance of so simple an alliance. But any choice on terms of state equality involves a major threat, whose magnitude was plainly illustrated last November [1948]. Had the election fallen to the House its action would, of course, have been determined by the dominant political allegiance of the newly chosen state delegations.   Despite the Democratic triumph, twenty delegations . . . [had] Republican majorities and three . . . [were] evenly divided. Without the states won by the Dixiecrat electors, there . . . [were] but twenty-one in which the Democrats . . . [controlled]. Twenty-five are needed for election. The congressmen of any one of the four Thurmond states could, therefore, have obstructed the reelection of the President [Truman].

What could have come from such a deadlock and efforts to resolve it?   Without a compromise acceptable to the dissenters, or a major Republican sacrifice, Mr. Barkley might . . . [have been] acting as President pursuant to the Twentieth Amendment. That might, indeed, have been the "compromise." Whatever might have happened, our system clearly cannot face third-party threats with assurance—should they win sufficient sectional adherence to make a solid showing in electoral votes. . . .

Proportional division as proposed by Lodge and Gossett undeniably would meet or mitigate these evils.   It would, of course, be totally unworkable if an electoral majority were still required, since minor candidates would normally win electoral votes.   But with election turning on plurality, the plan would meet most of the charges leveled at the present system.

The chance that a candidate with a substantial popular plurality may be defeated on electoral votes would be much reduced—though not eliminated (because of the state units and differences attending the equation of their voters and their electoral votes).   The reform would completely stop a voting block within a state from gaining influence transcending its own numbers.   It would deprive third-party states of the enormous possibility of forcing any choice upon a plane of state equality. Finally, and not least important, it would create major incentives for each party to campaign throughout the country, since minority support would mean electoral votes.

A problem is suggested by the fear that, since proportional division will give minor parties electoral votes, it may encourage fragmentation of the party system with the evils that much European history reveals. This danger has led some to defend present methods and others to support the old proposal of a poll by districts, as in choosing congressmen, on the theory that the minor parties will be washed out in the districts as now in the states. But this fear may depreciate unduly the bases of adherence to the two major parties. There is no reason why a scattering of electoral votes should give new parties more appeal or more capacity for growing than the popular votes they now obtain. What counts in this respect is the potentiality of victory. A mere electoral showing can do nothing more than change the mathematics of failure.

But proportional division would reduce the minor parties to their proper stature by depriving them of nuisance power. Under the reform, Henry Wallace could not have diverted all New York's forty-seven electoral votes to Dewey; he would have won slightly less than four of those votes himself. Governor Thurmond, having concentrated support in the states of small electorates, would have attained almost as many electoral votes throughout the country as he gained by present methods (36.8 instead of 39). But the momentous danger that such sectional dissent might bar a choice by electoral votes would have been removed.

Yet any method must take stock of the contingency that strong dissident parties may emerge. Should they be strong enough to win pluralities in many states, the present electoral method would collapse beneath their weight. All elections would then be settled in the House. Proportional division would permit multiple-party operation, but plurality election might bestow the presidency on a movement with a very narrow base. If it were governed by extremist elements, control of the executive would be a major threat.

This apprehension would be met by an insistence on a minimum percentage of the electoral votes to work election, for example, 35 per cent. Should no candidate have this much strength throughout the nation, congressional selection could be required, and—provided that it does not call for vote by states—it would be suitable. A choice by joint ballot of House and Senate—with each member granted equal voice—would safeguard all basic values, including the weight of each state in electoral votes. This method would, in the event supposed, require the perfection of a coalition in advance of a selection, provide opportunity to eliminate extremists, and produce a President likely to have sufficient strength with Congress for effective government. A change in this direction would improve the reform plan. . . .

To proportional division, there is, however, a surviving and perhaps insoluble objection of a magnitude commensurate with all merit the reform can claim. It is that the method would enormously reduce the influence of states with large electorates accustomed to a close division in their voting. Correlatively, it would raise the power of single-party states.

Though almost any election would establish this, the point was made most clearly in 1944. The twelve southern states polling a vote of 5,609,320 gave a plurality to Roosevelt of 2,263,270, which brought him 138 electoral votes as against none for his opponent. Division would have cut his lead to 65+, giving him 99+ to 33+ for Dewey and 4+ for minor candidates. The five states with the largest voting populations all have active party competition. They cast a total vote of 20,621,569, returning a Roosevelt plurality of 1,026,256, which gave him 135 electoral votes as against 25 for Dewey, an advantage of 110. But a division would have cut this lead to less than 8 producing 83+ for F.D.R. to 75+ for Dewey.

The point is made emphatically by the situation within individual states. California with 3,320,875 votes yielded Roosevelt a plurality of 475,599. Proportional division would have made this advantage worth less than 4 electoral votes. New York gave Roosevelt a lead of 316,591 on a vote of 6,316,790. Under division the electoral advantage would have been but slightly more than 2. Yet South Carolina with 103,375 votes and a Roosevelt preference of 86,054 would have produced an electoral lead of almost 7 votes. So Mississippi would have counted over 7 in return for a plurality of 154,773 among 180,080; and Texas, showing a majority of 630,180 out of 1,150,330, would have contributed a lead of almost 13.

What is involved is not alone that, under the division system, unity within a state gives sectional advantage. The states that have such unity are largely those in which there are the fewest voters in relation to the population that determines electoral votes (above the constitutional minimum of three). The combination of these factors would, therefore, enhance the inequality in voting influence that flows from the retention of state units and the electoral ratios. Thus a plurality within the single-party states would, on the figures stated, have had an average worth more than three times that given to a similar plurality in the largest states that have the keenest competition.

The impact of the change is shown by its probable effect on party practice. Where the conventions now emphasize the large and doubtful states, proportional division would inevitably turn them to the South—the Democrats seeking to hold their advantage, the Republicans to reduce what would be an overwhelming lead. But if the present emphasis presents the evils noted earlier, it has at least the virtue of its limitations. On the whole, it centers party thought on the needs and claims of the most numerous among us, making up for the cut in influence that the electoral system gives their individual votes. To shift this emphasis to the states with the smallest electorates would present comparable evils without comparable gain.

The answer given by the reform advocates is that proportional division would create party competition where it now is lacking and so pressures for enlarging the electorate; that this, above all else, would vitalize two-party politics in the states affected. But the change could work to solidify adherence to one party and intensify desire for restriction of the franchise to retain the larger influence solidarity would yield. The other states would then have no defense but imitation—in the same way that states that first chose their electors on a district basis soon felt impelled by those that would not risk division to adopt the methods that made unity the rule.

Any such increase in single-party states would hardly be an advance. The function of the parties is to work out coalitions that command sufficient nation-wide support to win elections and provide effective government. Nothing would thwart that function more effectively than a consolidation along merely sectional lines. Should the one-party states desire party competition and believe that they will get it by proportional division, they are now free to choose the method for themselves. If it produces the results predicted, then we shall know that it can safely be decreed for all.

Yet it would be a misfortune if disagreement on the merit of proportional division should obstruct the abolition of electors and the adoption of a Federal guarantee of popular participation in the choice. And the 1948 election may have taught sufficient lesson to make possible one further change of great importance: the elimination of the vote by states upon the failure of electoral majority and the substitution of a vote per capita by members of both houses—preferably limited to choice between the two leading candidates. Were all these changes made, we might await with greater confidence a day when proportional division may offer a clearer gain than it does now.

FERGUSON ASKS SOME QUESTIONS [10]

I recognize that the present electoral college is obsolete and inconvenient. It involves the risk of throwing a presidential election into the House. It contains glaring inequalities and it fails to reflect with absolute accuracy patterns of voting behavior. But it has served us well. And before we abandon it I believe that we should know exactly what any substitute would signify.

A principal argument advanced on behalf of this constitutional amendment is that it will strengthen the two-party system in the United States.

[10] From extension of remarks by Senator Homer Ferguson (Republican, Michigan), March 9, 1949. In *Election of President and Vice President;* hearings, February 23-May 3, 1949, before a subcommittee of the Senate Judiciary Committee on S. Joint Resolution 2, 81st Congress, 1st session. The Committee. Washington, D.C. 1949. p513-4.

I think the two-party system is the great genius of the American political organism. By vertical alignment it isolates the lunatic fringes, as one keen observer has stated, and it permits the joining of more closely aligned elements into an efficient working machine, although delicately balanced. I think we may reasonably require every assurance that such a mechanism will not be upset before we embark on any departures from the present scheme.

There are further questions on which I believe we should have some penetrating and original thinking. . . .

1. If a constitutional amendment were adopted, guaranteeing electoral votes to every candidate according to popular votes, would candidates be likely to argue that states must put them on the ballot since presidential elections are now Federal and not state contests? In short, would Federal regulation of presidential elections be likely to follow, to protect the right of the candidate to his share of the popular vote? Why grant him an electoral share if states can keep him off the ballot?

2. Are presidential campaigns likely to be more costly under the proposed change? Or, would less money be spent in the big states and more in other areas, without increasing the total cost? Would we have different campaign techniques and what would their change mean to different areas and to individual voters?

3. By offering an incentive to see power grow in the electoral vote, would multiple parties be encouraged? Formerly, splinter parties were stopped at the state and regional level; would they now retain their identity, resist being swallowed up in the major parties and bid for power on their own? Is the incentive of electoral vote too weak to encourage splinter parties or will it have a tendency to encourage them?

4. What has been the experience in other countries with regard to multiple parties?

5. We have had a number of minority Presidents. Will this tendency increase under the new proposal?

6. By translating popular votes into electoral votes under the unit rule, the tendency was to cancel out smaller candidates having less than a plurality and to give the winning candidate

a national character by a larger electoral vote. Would the new proposal change this by accentuating the minority status of a winner?

7. Which is the greater threat to the American system: nuisance minorities under a two-party umbrella or multiple parties in their own?

8. If multiple parties could develop under the new system, could they bid for a share in national government power even though they do not succeed in electing a President? Today we have many bipartisan boards and commissions in the Federal Government; might the new proposal send this into the direction of multipartisan boards with block pressure for concessions? Would not multiple parties, even if they failed to elect their presidential candidate, be expected to elect members to Congress, and what would that effect have on congressional organization?

9. Would the new proposal push the representative system in the direction of national popularity contests and thus into "bread and circus" politics?

10. Would the new proposal lead to the setting up of puppet parties in states solid to one party or another for the purpose of drawing off electoral votes from the major parties? Minor parties do this now; would the tendency be encouraged?

11. There is general agreement that the new proposal would break up the South. Do reason and history support the view that the Republican party, as the existing alternate party, would move in and get a strong share of southern votes to revivify the two-party system, or would the break-up lead to third parties in the South?

12. Would electoral votes under the new system be free of voting inequalities such as now prevail?

13. The amendment proposes to compute fractional electoral votes only to one-thousandth unless a more detailed computation would change the result of the selection. Is this intended solely to apply in case of a tie? Is it possible that a peculiar breakage of fractions might, by a further projection, change the results? If so, can these breakages be anticipated, and how should projections be treated? . . .

The question before us is not one that goes just to the obsoleteness of the electoral college. On that there is general agreement. The question goes to what an alternative might bring, and on that question we need all possible light.

REPUBLICAN OPPOSITION VIEWS [11]

Senator Lodge says that Senate Joint Resolution 2 will reduce or eliminate the possibility of a candidate getting an electoral vote majority despite receiving only a minority of the popular vote.

On the contrary, his amendment would make this possibility, which has occurred only three times in the nation's history—in 1824, 1876, and 1888—a probability, if not a certainty.

It also will destroy the Republican party, of which Senator Lodge is a member, and the two-party system, which is the foundation of the government, replacing it by a multiparty system.

The Lodge amendment trades large blocks of electoral votes in states other than the Solid South, commonly carried by Republicans, for almost negligible electoral votes gained in the southern states.

Each electoral vote won in the South represents an average of 40,000 popular votes against an average of 110,000 votes per electoral vote in the remaining thirty-seven states of the North and Central states.

To all practical purposes, this will make a Republican presidential victory impossible as long as the Solid South remains solid in its voting habits.

Striking evidence as to the operation of the Lodge plan is shown by applying the formula of the pending resolution to the four elections of Franklin D. Roosevelt in 1932, 1936, 1940, and 1944.

[11] From a statement by Basil Brewer, publisher of the New Bedford (Mass.) *Standard Times*, March 9, 1949. In *Election of President and Vice President;* hearings, February 23-May 3, 1949, before a subcommittee of the Senate Judiciary Committee on S. Joint Resolution 2. 81st Congress, 1st session. The Committee. Washington, D.C, 1949. p54-69.

In 1932, under the Lodge plan, Hoover would have been 84 electoral votes behind Roosevelt in the eleven states of the South, each electoral vote that year representing an average of 30,260 popular votes.

To overcome this Roosevelt electoral vote lead in the South and win the election, Hoover would have had to get a lead of 85 electoral votes in the remaining thirty-seven states, where each electoral vote that year represented 85,580 popular votes, on the average.

In other words, to be elected under the Lodge plan, Hoover would have had to pile up a popular vote lead of 7,274,300 votes in the thirty-seven states of the North for a North-South plurality of 4,925,652 votes.

Two electoral votes less (100,000 to 200,000 popular votes) would have meant defeat.

Under such conditions, Hoover, with a popular vote plurality of almost five million would have been defeated by Roosevelt with a majority of the electoral vote. Never in the history of the country were such wide discrepancies between popular vote and electoral vote possible.

The elections of 1936, 1940, and 1944 show the same possibilities.

In 1936, under the Lodge plan, Roosevelt would have had a lead in the Solid South of 84 electoral votes over Alf Landon, a year when an electoral vote in the South represented 33,570 popular votes.

To overcome this lead, plus one, and win the election, Landon would have had to gain a popular vote lead of 8,352,100 in the remaining thirty-seven states, for a North-South popular vote lead of 5,783,442.

Two electoral votes less (100,000 to 200,000 popular votes) would have given Roosevelt the election by an electoral vote lead of one, and with Landon having a popular vote lead of more than 5.5 million, under the Lodge plan.

Similarly in 1940, under the Lodge amendment, it would have been possible for Roosevelt to have had an electoral vote lead and been elected, with Willkie having a popular vote lead of more than 5.5 million.

In 1944, under the Lodge plan, Dewey could have had a popular vote lead of approximately 5.25 million and been defeated by Roosevelt having a lead of one in the electoral college. . . .

Senator Lodge speculates that his plan would lead to more party activity of the Republicans in the South, and in this hope he is somewhat encouraged by his colleague, Representative Gossett, of Texas, who says he would welcome more Republican votes in the South, meaning, I am sure, so long as there were not too many of them. . . .

This is no proper place to discuss the voting problems of the South, except to point out the eleven states of the South are electing 127 presidential electors with approximately one third the popular vote required for the same number elsewhere. . . .

The Associated Press quoted Senator Lodge on February 23 as arguing his amendment would make the popular vote count, by abolishing the electoral college's "traditional unit voting rule."

How about the five million popular-vote majority by which Senator Lodge's own party could conceivably lead, only to be defeated by another party's lead in the electoral vote spearheaded by an irreconcilable Solid South, as previously discussed?

Would not these five million votes be "lost"?

As a matter of fact . . . in every election where one man is concerned, such as the election of a President, no votes cast, except for the winner, count, and all others are in that sense lost. The Lodge-Gossett plan merely transfers the "wasted votes" from the state to the national level.

Apparently completely overlooked are the unexplored psychologies involved in the Lodge plan in small states like Senator McCarran's state, Nevada, which has sixty thousand voters and three electoral votes, and is traditionally Democratic by a narrow margin.

In a normal presidential year, Nevada's electoral vote would be divided under the Lodge plan $1\frac{3}{8}$ Republican and $1\frac{5}{8}$ Democratic, for a Democratic electoral vote lead of $\frac{1}{4}$. . . .

As a part-time resident of Nevada, I know something of Nevadans, who feel three electoral votes are very few for a state so large. It is possible both Democrats and Republicans might be discouraged in voting if success either way meant a lead of only $\frac{1}{2}$, $\frac{1}{4}$, $\frac{1}{8}$, or 1/16 of an electoral vote.

And, finally, Senator Lodge, co-sponsor of this bill, argues his amendment "will eliminate the possibility of a President being elected by the House of Representatives, when no candidate gets a clear-cut majority of electoral votes."

I am a little surprised at the Senator urging this point, for the way the Senator's plan eliminates the possibility of action by the House of Representatives is to give the election to whoever has the electoral vote plurality, by-passing the House, no matter how small is the electoral vote or plurality. . . .

Under the Lodge plan, every party to an election is allowed that party's share of the electoral vote, Democratic, Republican, Prohibition, Socialist, Communist—first at the state, then at the national level. No votes are "lost" in the Lodge sense at the state level; no parties are lost sight of, at state or national level.

Unquestionably the Lodge plan would first eliminate the Republican party. Then would go on in real earnest the attrition of the Democratic party, as cleavage after cleavage followed the inability of that party to satisfy the demands of widely conflicting ideologies and interests. . . .

You cannot destroy the Republican party without destroying the two-party system. You cannot destroy the two-party system without destroying ultimately the Democratic party or reducing it to a minority position, surrounded by other minority parties maneuvering and trading with one another in the well-nigh hopeless task of trying to establish workable coalitions. . . .

When, under the Lodge plan, a minority party has grown to the stature of a substantial electoral vote, will such party be satisfied to be without legislative representation or with only such representation as it may acquire here and there where local strength may give it a member of the House of Representatives?

Or will some intelligent and ambitious politician see in the strong minority party, represented only by electoral votes, a chance to win distinction and position by championing its cause, and make a fight to secure legislative representation by the same formula which enabled it to obtain electoral vote representation, by proportional voting?

Under the Lodge plan the voting for President becomes federalized. There no longer is voting by states as has existed for 160 years. Will the state still be allowed to determine the qualifications of its electors as specified in the Constitution? Or will the courts conclude that this amendment, which guarantees each party its share of the electoral votes at the state level, by the same token must guarantee this party the right to appear on the ballot of the state, regardless of the action of the state? . . .

Senator Lodge says his bill will enable the Republican party to invade the southern states and increase the Republican vote. It is by this plan he hopes to offset the handicap of his party, to some extent, in the Solid South, where on the average an electoral vote represents some 40,000 or less popular votes, as against an average of 110,000 in the remaining thirty-seven states.

Obviously such Republican votes cannot come from the tight Democratic majority in these states, which, facing the Truman civil-rights program, still refused to vote Republican. Such votes then could come only from the nonvoting population of the South.

Already the Constitution, in Article XIV, Section 2, [Amendments] provides:

When the right to vote at any election for the choice of electors for President and Vice President of the United States, Representatives in Congress, the executive and judicial officers of a State, or the members of the legislature thereof, is denied to any of the male inhabitants of such State, being twenty-one years of age, and citizens of the United States, or in any way abridged, except for participation in rebellion, or other crime, the basis of representation therein shall be reduced in the proportion which the number of such male citizens shall bear to the whole number of male citizens twenty-one years of age in such State.

Do our friends of the South wish to face the additional pressure for enforcement of this provision which the Lodge campaign for votes in the South would ensure as well as the very real risk the electoral college "reform" might lead to Federal control of elections?

FOR THE COUDERT PROPOSAL [12]

The concept of the electoral college as the counterpart of Congress in the articulation of Federal and national electoral power was destroyed by political leaders of the larger party in each of the states. To win all of the electoral power in a state these political leaders had things rearranged so that all presidential electors ran for election on general state-wide tickets. This is the arrangement that permits the entire electoral vote of a state to go to the presidential candidate of one party by as little as one vote plurality. This practice is the source of the complaints against our present electoral system. This is the situation sought to be corrected. I don't believe there are very many among the American people who want to change violently the structure of our government, and I am certain that the sponsors of the Lodge-Gossett amendment are not among that number.

I am equally certain that the Coudert electoral reform plan [H. Joint Resolution 1, 83d Congress, 1st session] will make the electoral college the exact counterpart of a joint session of the Senate and the House of Representatives. It provides:

Section 1. Each state shall choose a number of electors of the President and Vice President, equal to the whole number of Senators and Representatives to which the state may be entitled in the Congress, in the same manner as its Senators and Representatives are chosen. . . .

The effect of this provision would be to put an end to the prevailing practice in the states of choosing all of their presidential electors by the general state-wide ticket system. Rather, only the two Federal electors, corresponding to each states' two senators, would be elected on a state-wide basis, unless, as in some states, some of the representatives are elected at large; and the national electors, corresponding to the representatives in Congress, would be elected in congressional districts, or at large in a few cases.

[12] From a letter by J. Harvie Williams, executive vice president, Committee on Electoral Reform, to Representative Frederick R. Coudert, Jr. (Republican, New York). In *Amend Constitution to Abolish Electoral College System;* hearings, April 18 and 20, 1951, before Subcommittee no 1 of the House Judiciary Committee on H. Joint Resolutions 11, 14, 19, 89, 90, 109 and 205. 82d Congress, 1st session. Superintendent of Documents. Washington, D.C. 1951. p68-70.

Adoption of the Coudert amendment would have these important political effects:

1. Divide each state's electoral power among the parties on the same basis that its congressional power is divided among them. Thus national parties would have electoral power commensurate with their congressional power—an ideal situation.

2. Give the presidency to any party that won a bare majority (218) of the seats in the House, and won a bare majority of the states (25) with two electors each, for a total of 268 electoral votes, or won more congressional districts and carried fewer states.

3. The President and the whole Congress would have exactly the same constituency cast up in the same form. Pressure groups of all kinds would have the same weight in electing the President that they have in electing the whole membership of the House and Senate. There would be no basis for an ideological conflict between the President and the Congress when both were of such close political complexion.

4. Both large and small states would have their political weight properly divided among the parties in the election of the President.

5. States having large blocs of doubtful electoral votes would no longer be the exclusive sources of party candidates for President, although they would continue to have the largest delegations at the nominating conventions.

6. New York's 47 doubtful electoral votes under the present system would be reduced to a doubtful 12 under the Coudert amendment, since only 10 of its 45 House seats (43 before 1932) have changed their party representation since 1920. The two Federal electors would always be doubtful. New York would continue to be a dominant state, but its dominance would not be overwhelming. The same would be true of other large states like Pennsylvania, Ohio, Illinois, and California.

It is clear, then, that the Coudert amendment conforms squarely with the established structure of our national government, that it would almost exactly balance the electoral and congressional power of the political parties, and thus would eliminate the basis of the present ideological conflict between the President and the Congress—a conflict that will doom our form of government if it is not soon ended.

It should be noted that the Coudert amendment maintains the requirement of a majority of the electoral vote for the election of the President; and it should be emphasized that the majority requirement is the primary basis of our two-party political system. Under the Coudert amendment, when no candidate for President or Vice President received a majority of the electoral vote the final choices would be made by a joint session of Congress voting as a single body, from among the persons having the three highest numbers of votes on the lists of those voted for for each office. Three fourths of the combined membership of the Senate and the House would be required for a quorum.

AGAINST ELECTION BY DISTRICTS [13]

It has been suggested that we do away with the state unit vote and substitute a system of selecting presidential electors by districts in each state [the Coudert proposal].

Such a plan is discredited by our past history. It would retain the worst features of the present method.

First, it would preserve the presidential elector who never has and never can cast a vote that would accurately reflect the will of the people of the district from which he is elected.

Second, it would continue the present provision which denies the right of the people to vote directly for President.

Third, it would preserve the unit vote in a form that would still disfranchise all minorities. It would deny any representation to minority votes within the district that selected him and therefore disfranchise minority votes in every district in the country.

Fourth, it would set up a system of districts that would tend to revive the gerrymandering practices that have so discredited many legislatures in the past by their brutal exercise of political

[13] From testimony by former Representative Clarence L. Lea (Republican, California). April 18, 1951. In *Amend Constitution to Abolish Electoral College System;* hearings, April 18 and 20, 1951, before Subcommittee no 1 of the House Judiciary Committee on H. Joint Resolutions 11, 14, 19, 89, 90, 109 and 205. 82d Congress, 1st session. Superintendent of Documents. Washington, D.C. 1951. p10-46.

power to prevent minority parties from getting just credit in the election.

Fifth, the district system of election is merely an attempt to palliate but provides no real constructive remedy for the evils of the present system.

Sixth, the great inequality between the populations of different districts would, under district selection, provide impossible inequalities in the voting rights of the people within the states.

The district selection of a presidential elector is condemned not only by the gerrymandering of districts that has heretofore prevailed, but also by the unequal population of districts, whether or not gerrymandering has anything to do with their size.

This great inequality in the size of districts was recognized by the President in his message to Congress on January 9, 1951, in reference to reapportionment under the recent census, the President stated:

> Over the years, widespread discrepancies have grown up between the populations of the various congressional districts. While some variation is inevitable, the extreme differences that now exist can and should be corrected. For example, there is one state in which, according to the 1950 census, the smallest district has a population of under 175,000 and the largest district has a population exceeding 900,000. In many states, there are differences of two or three hundred thousand people between the smallest and largest existing districts in the state. While about half of the congressional districts throughout the country are between 300,000 and 400,000 in population, there are some fifty districts with a population of 250,000 or less, and, at the other extreme, some fifty districts with a population of 450,000 or over. . . .
>
> Such defects in our system of congressional districts obstruct the effective operation of the democratic principles on which our whole Government rests. It is fundamental to the whole structure of the Constitution that all citizens have equal representation, so far as practicable, in the House of Representatives. . . .
>
> In terms of the present census, assuming an average district of about 350,000 persons, a percentage permitting a range of about 50,000 above and below that figure would probably allow for the practical difficulties which state legislatures face in drawing up district boundaries.

The fundamental vice of the presidential elector is that he prevents the representation of minority voters. Whether or not he be selected by state units or by district units the evils are fundamentally the same.

The presidential elector is selected by part of the voters of the state. He represents them, and no others. The presidential elector by his mere selection denies representation to all minority voters within the state, be they members of the Democratic, or Republican, or third party.

To select electors by districts gives no actual promise of any improvement above the present system of selection. Instead of having 48 unit votes, as at present, we would have 483.

If such a method of election were established and we could conceive a popular vote in each state on a common level within that state, every state would produce a solid electoral vote in favor of one party or the other. True, as a practical matter, the establishment of electoral districts within the states might result in more division of electoral votes within some states, but would give no assurance whatever that the aggregate result would be any better than at present.

In one respect the present plan of counting state votes as a unit is decidedly preferable to the district system of selection. The state unit vote makes gerrymandering of districts impossible. The selection of electors by districts would open the way for vicious state gerrymandering of electoral districts to serve wrongful partisan ends. Thus a new means of suppressing minority votes would be injected into our electoral system without any counteracting benefits.

President Benjamin Harrison has been quoted as saying that one reason for the adoption of the unit system in voting was to eliminate gerrymandering of districts in presidential elections. Whether or not that statement is accurate, it is, I think, unquestionably true that the state unit vote does have that advantage over the district system of selection.

Gerrymandering has been described as a "product of human cupidity and desire to gain power." The unit vote originated in the same illegitimate purpose of dominant political parties in the state to grab votes that rightfully belonged to their opponents. . . .

The Constitution properly provided electoral votes, allotted primarily on a basis of population, as the measure of the right of each state to participate in the election of the President. It failed to anticipate the time when the people of the country would, on their own account, want to select the President.

In view of the great variety of conditions that prevail in our widely separated forty-eight states, it is utterly impractical to attempt to devise any satisfactory plan of election that does not provide for a division of the state votes. Then, too, that division must give equal recognition to every vote lawfully cast within the state so that it will be given its proper credit in the final count that determines the election.

This requires the elimination of the presidential elector. No difference how selected, he never has been and never will be able to cast a vote for President that will accurately reflect the divided will of the people of the state from which he was selected.

The presidential elector is an obvious obstruction to any proper system of election and must be eliminated.

TWO CHIEF PROPOSALS COMPARED [14]

Beginning now with the mode of distributing a state's electoral votes between the several candidates for President, I would remark that under the existing arrangements there is scarcely ever any distribution at all. In the ordinary course the candidate who receives a plurality of a state's popular vote receives the whole of its electoral vote. That is because in every state the presidential electors—men without an independent judgment, mere agents of their constituents, pledged, before they are chosen, to give their votes according to the will of those who choose them—are appointed on the general ticket system. Under that system every voter in each state votes for every elector to which his state is entitled. Since a plurality is sufficient to elect it follows almost automatically that the political party with the greatest number of votes secures the appointment of its entire slate of electors and consequently secures the whole of the state's electoral vote.

[14] From study by Lucius Wilmerding, Jr., Institute for Advanced Studies, Princeton, N.J. Included in *Amend Constitution to Abolish Electoral College System;* hearings, April 18 and 20, 1951, before Subcommittee no 1 of the House Judiciary Committee on H. Joint Resolutions 11, 14, 19, 89, 90, 109 and 205. 82d Congress, 1st session. Superintendent of Documents. Washington, D.C. 1951. p78-91.

This is the evil which both the Gossett and the Coudert amendments propose to remedy. That it is an evil I have no doubt. I know that two arguments have been advanced in favor of the general ticket system or, to speak more generally, in favor of any system which permits a state to consolidate its electoral votes. One is based on a political calculation; a party will gain or lose more by the breaking up of the Solid South than it will lose or gain by the breaking up of the doubtful North. This argument seems to me unworthy of examination; if a party can win an election only through the accidents of mathematics, then perhaps it does not deserve to win.

The second argument is more honorable. It is grounded on the proposition, indisputable so far as it goes, that a large state should have a greater weight in the choice of a President than a small state. New York is entitled under the rules of the Constitution to 47 electoral votes, Mississippi to 9; but suppose that the votes of New York are given to the two parties in the ratio of 24 to 23, those of Mississippi in the ratio of 8 to 1—the net weight of New York in the election is one, that of Mississippi is seven. But can we say that, by this token, Mississippi has become seven times as important as New York? I think not. The gross weight of a state, and that is all that we should look at, is not reduced by being distributed. In the given instance New York remains much more important than Mississippi, even its minority has more weight than all of Mississippi. Let me put the matter another way. The election of a President is a joint venture of the people of the United States rather than a joint venture of the several states in their corporate capacities. In this view it is perfectly proper that the minorities in some states should combine with the majorities in others to form a majority of the whole. It is very improper that the majority in any state should seize the votes of its minority, add them to its own, and so give itself an electorial advantage which it has neither earned nor deserved. . . .

All these considerations, taken together, seem to me to prove one thing: that something should be done to break the power of the several states to combine and concentrate their electoral votes upon a single candidate. What should be done is, however, another question. And the answer to it is not obvious.

At first blush it might seem that the most practicable solution would be to abolish the whole electoral voting system—the electoral votes as well as the presidential electors—and to commit the choice of a President to the people of the United States voting at large. But the idea is visionary, and I shall not pause to examine its merits and demerits. Under the electoral voting system prescribed by the Constitution each state is allotted a number of electors proportional to its population, plus two; these two additional electors give to the small states a weight relatively greater than that of the large states. Any proposal which would result in depriving the small states of their privileged position could not pass the Senate. It is, therefore, idle to discuss it. A reform, to stand any chance of adoption, must be based on the retention of the electoral allotments to each state, including the two-vote credit. . . .

The Gossett amendment . . . does away with the state electoral colleges but keeps the state electoral votes; these it distributes between the several candidates for President upon the principle of proportion. An individual who has received 40 per cent of a state's popular vote receives 40 per cent of its electoral vote, and so on. The calculation is carried to three decimal places in the attempt to achieve exact mathematical accuracy.

The merits of this proposal are very easy to see. It gives to every political grouping of voters in the national election a weight as nearly proportional to its mass as the present unequal weighting of the states permits. It avoids the seizure of minority votes by majorities. It reduces the size of the electoral swings which may be caused by accident, fraud, or the power of minor parties. It destroys in some measure the political advantages of the large doubtful states. It would revive political activity in the sure states.

Its demerits are not so obvious. And yet I think they exist. They can best be brought out by comparing the proposed system with the district system.

The district system is based upon the proposition that each equal mass of persons—comprising voters and nonvoters alike—

is entitled to an equal voice in the choice of a President; the proportional system is based upon the proposition that such equal aggregation of actual voters is to have an equal voice and that nonvoters are to have no voice. Of the two principles, I think that the former is the sounder. I can see no reason why an equal mass should be deprived of its equal voice merely because a lesser rather than a larger proportion of its total numbers actually goes to the polls. . . .

Some case, indeed, might be made for the proportional system against the district system, if it could be shown that the one is more likely than the other to result in the election of the real choice of the people. But I conceive that this cannot be done. In the first place the two systems are incommensurable. The district system seeks to ascertain the will of the majority of the people—of all the people, not merely of the active voters. The proportional system limits its investigation to the opinions of the latter. In the second place, the proportional system can never really reflect the nation-wide popular vote with exactitude. The two electoral votes allotted to each state regardless of population together with differing proportions of the total population which exercise the suffrage in the different states destroy the correspondence. . . .

It is not true, what many writers have alleged, that the vast majority of the framers of the Constitution distrusted the people, feared popular elections, and in general agreed with George Mason when he said that "it would be as unnatural to refer the choice of a proper character for Chief Magistrate to the people as it would to refer a trial of colors to a blind man." James Wilson, who first proposed the scheme of electors, apparently regarded it as equivalent to an election by the people. When it was finally adopted, Madison had no hesitancy in saying that "The President is now to be elected by the people." . . .

For an explanation of the origin of the electors we must look elsewhere than to imagined distrust upon the part of the founding fathers in the popular principle of election. If we read the debates in the Federal Convention, we cannot but see that the electoral system was advocated not so much as a means of correcting the judgment of the people, and never as a means of ignoring or superseding it, but as a device for getting over the difficulty arising out of the disproportion of qualified voters in the North and South. According to Madison:

There was one difficulty, however, of a serious nature attending an immediate choice by the people. The right of suffrage was much more diffusive in the northern than the southern states; and the latter could have no influence in the election on the score of the Negroes. The substitution of electors obviated this difficulty. . . .

The electors have in fact been useful in a number of ways; they may, especially if the general ticket is gotten rid of, be useful in others. In the first place, they have served to connect the President and the Vice President, so as to make it almost impossible to elect a President of one political party and a Vice President of another. . . .

Under the present arrangements this advantage of electors may be thought to be a small one. The operation of the general ticket system has been such as invariably to give some candidate a majority of the electoral vote. No combination of minority parties could affect the result. But if the general ticket were to be broken up—either by the district system or by proportional voting—occasions might frequently arise when majority opposition to a plurality candidate might make itself felt. On such occasions the advantage mentioned by Madison would be very considerable. . . .

In the Lodge-Gossett amendment of last year, as originally introduced, the person having the greatest number of electoral votes for President was to be President, regardless of how small that number might be in relation to the total electoral vote; no provision at all was made for taking the sense of the nation in cases where the electoral vote might be scattered in very small parcels among several candidates. The Gossett resolution of this year makes a plurality of at least 40 per cent of the total vote necessary to a final choice by the people; the Coudert resolution sticks to the present constitutional requirement of an absolute majority.

That some percentage of the total vote should be fixed as necessary to a final choice by the people seems to me fairly plain. In cases where no candidate has received a very large vote, the person receiving the greatest number of votes may not be in any true sense of the word the choice of the nation. It is conceivable that he might, in fact, be totally obnoxious to a great majority of the nation. . . .

Turning now to the mode of voting in Congress when the election devolves upon it, I note that both resolutions reject the present mode of voting by states in the House of Representatives and substitute a mode of voting by heads in the two Houses sitting in joint session. . . .

The majority of the House of Representatives, when taken by states, is liable to be very different than when taken by heads. If an election were to be thrown into the House under the present rule it is conceivable that the result would be not to confirm the sense of the majority of the people but of the minority. . . .

The only question which I would raise here is whether it might not be better to give the eventual choice to the House of Representatives alone. It seems proper that in the election of a President the popular principle alone should prevail—unqualified by the so-called Federal principle. . . .

The Gossett and Coudert amendments disagree in one other important respect. The first would confine the choice of President by Congress to "the persons having the two highest numbers of electoral votes"; the second would extend the choices to "the persons having the highest numbers, not exceeding three."

The question of three or two is not perhaps very important. The advantage of three, as Madison once pointed out, is that "it not unfrequently happens that the candidate third on the list of votes would in a question with either of the two first outvote him, and, consequently, be the real preference of the voters." But on the other hand, it is easier to obtain "a prompt and quiet decision by Congress" with two candidates before them than with three. Madison himself considered that this second advantage outweighed the first. And so do I.

SMATHERS PROPOSES THREE CHANGES [15]

Efforts to revise and reform the election machinery of this nation should be nonpartisan, or bipartisan. Both our major

[15] From remarks by Senator George Smathers (Democrat, Florida) in the United States Senate, January 6, 1953. *Congressional Record.* 99:(daily)161-2. January 7, 1953. Reprinted by permission.

political parties should be interested in achieving changes in the direction to which my proposals point, and no particular significance should be attached to the failure of both conventions last summer to endorse the National Primary Plan because much of the dissatisfaction with the present method of selecting nominees for President and Vice President is based upon the firsthand knowledge of the operations of conventions—a knowledge general throughout the country for which television is to be thanked.

This is the fifth year in which I have urged the Congress to move toward election reforms. Those of us—and there are many in this body—who fervently believe in such reforms feel no discouragement over previous failures. Heretofore we did not have television on our side to show the American people the complete inadequacy and downright evil of the present convention system of nominating Presidents. We have not heretofore had such widespread interest in the changing of many of our election procedures. But the American people by the aid of television and spurred on by recent elections have awakened, and are now urgently requesting that we, the Congress—the only ones who can do anything about this situation—get busy and act. If there is any doubt on the part of senators of the attitude of the American people toward these proposals, I direct senators' attention to the most recent Gallup Poll which appeared in various papers on Sunday, January 4. The poll shows that over 73 per cent of the people are anxious to have the archaic practice of selecting a presidential candidate put in the coffin and under the ground forever. The poll shows that the public favors a nation-wide nominating primary by overwhelming majority and by an ever-increasing percentage.

The American public is also anxious to change the present electoral college procedure, recognizing it as ancient, undemocratic and dangerous. According to Mr. Gallup's figures, every two out of three people in the United States would like to see the Congress of the United States get busy and change the electoral college system. On November 22, 1952, the able Senator from Arkansas, Senator Fulbright, and myself, without previous consultation and without knowledge of the other's thinking, issued statements on that day expressing our belief that the present law is unsatisfactory which permits a Vice President to succeed to the presidency upon the death of the President of the United States, and to hold that presidency for the balance of the four-year term. This tenure of the Vice President has, on more than one occasion, been almost the full four-year term. . . . It is clear that the founding fathers of our governmental system intended that the Vice President should be only the "caretaker" of the office of the President until such time as the people could expeditiously go about the business of electing a new President. The average citizen approves of that conclusion if this most recent Gallup Poll is anywhere near correct, for it reflects that 61 per cent of the citizens of the United States favor a change in the present system. Therefore, today, Mr. President, I am again introducing a resolution calling for constitutional amendments to effect changes in our election procedures.

The first constitutional change would establish a nation-wide primary for the nominating of party candidates for President. This is not a new proposal. As a matter of fact, Woodrow Wilson recommended nation-wide primaries in his message to the Congress in 1913. [The late] Senator George Norris of Nebraska . . . advocated a somewhat similar proposal. . . . Senator [Paul] Douglas [of Illinois] . . . last year . . . introduced a proposal which . . . urged nominating primaries by the states on a permissive basis, rather than effecting a constitutional amendment making nation-wide primaries mandatory.

The second part of this resolution would abolish the electoral college system of electing the President and Vice President. It would establish a system under which the electoral votes of each of the states would be divided among candidates on the basis of the percentage of popular votes received by each candidate in the states. This proposal was most recently identified with the former able Senator from Massachusetts, Mr. [Henry Cabot] Lodge and the former distinguished Congressman from Texas, Mr. Ed Gossett. This proposed change in the electoral college procedure passed the Senate in 1950 but failed to pass in the House of Representatives.

The third proposal in this resolution which I am today introducing provides, that when a President dies, or otherwise becomes incapacitated to serve as President, that the Vice President succeed to the presidency but hold that office only until the next general election, providing the next general election is more than ninety days away. . . .

We cannot continue to limp along in this year of 1953—with all its marvelous means of communication and education and with an alert and an aroused citizenry—on the same old election procedures which have on several occasions in the past permitted a man to become President even though he did not receive the largest popular vote, and has permitted political leaders and backroom barons to nominate and select presidential candidates.

I do not claim authorship or proprietorship of any of these proposals. Most of them have been discussed on forums, in debate classes, and even in the Congress in the past years. They belong to all of us. The recent Gallup poll proves that the citizens of your state and mine know of these ideas and are anxious that we cease debating them academically and make of them a reality. These proposals should be treated in bipartisan manner for they do not concern just Republicans or just Democrats. They are a matter of vital concern to the strength and well-being of our entire democracy.

HOW THE TEN-YEAR LIMIT WORKS [16]

There can be third terms in the future. But no President after Mr. Truman, under the amended Constitution, can serve more than ten years in the White House. . . .

The Constitution now says that no President who has served more than half of the four-year term of his predecessor can have more than one additional term. A man who serves two years or less of his predecessor's term thus could be elected twice, to two terms of his own, for a possible total of ten years. . . .

If a Vice President succeeds to the presidency just after mid-term for a President . . . he would be entitled to try for two

[16] From ''We've Been Asked: When Presidents Must Quit.'' *United States News & World Report*, an independent weekly news magazine on national and international affairs, published at Washington, D.C. 32:66. February 22, 1952. Copyright 1952, by United States News Publishing Company. Reprinted by permission.

additional terms. If Mr. Truman, for example, had taken over in 1947, instead of 1945, there would have been no question about his right to run for two additional terms. . . .

Two full terms of four years each are to be standard under the Constitution, if a President is able to get reelected. In most cases, the limit will be eight years, with voters being given a chance for a change after four years. The Amendment reads:

No person shall be elected to the office of President more than twice, and no person who has held the office of President, or acted as President, for more than two years of a term to which some other person was elected President shall be elected to the office of President more than once.

Can a man run for Vice President only twice, too? That's not involved. The Twenty-second Amendment . . . limits only the number of times a person can be elected President. It places no restrictions on running for the vice-presidency.

IF A PRESIDENT-ELECT DIES [17]

If the President-elect should die before members of the electoral college meet in the capitals of their states . . . these electors would select the next President. Actually, the Constitution does not direct that presidential electors be bound to vote for any particular person, but leaves them freedom of choice to select whom they wish. . . .

Who are the electors? They are men and women who are active in party affairs in their communities. Some are doctors and lawyers or members of other professions, or businessmen, often with strong likings for individual leaders in their parties. They cannot be, the Constitution says, members of Congress or federal officeholders.

Wouldn't the [Vice President-elect] automatically become President-designate if the President-elect died? Not if the President-elect died before the electors meet. . . . The Constitu-

[17] From *United States News & World Report*, an independent weekly news magazine on national and international affairs, published at Washington, D.C. 33:84. November 14, 1952. Copyright 1952, United States News Publishing Company. Reprinted by permission.

tion does not say so, nor does any law of Congress. But the Twentieth Amendment to the Constitution, adopted in 1933, says that if the President-elect dies—between the meeting of members of the electoral college and inauguration day, January 20—then the Vice President-elect would become President. . . .

If electors considered a new man as President, who would advise them? They would not have to take the advice of anyone or any group. But it is likely that they would be guided by the advice of the Republican National Committee. A precedent for this may have been set in 1912 when the losing nominee for Vice President on the Republican ticket, James Sherman, died just before the election. The Republican National Committee directed the Republican electors—there were only eight of them—to vote for Nicholas Murray Butler for Vice President. This they did.

What if both men on the winning ticket died before inauguration day? If that happened before the . . . meetings of the electors, they would select both a President-elect and a Vice President-elect. Under the Constitution, they could pick anyone.

If both the President-elect and the Vice President-elect should die after the meeting of the electors and before inauguration, there is a definite rule on succession. First in line would be the Speaker of the House, who is in the role of a sort of second Vice President. . . . Next in line is the President pro tempore of the Senate. Then follow in line of succession members of the Cabinet, beginning with the Secretary of State. But it is not likely that Congress will be found without a qualified Speaker or President pro tempore at one time.

Have the electors ever had to pick a new man as President? No. But, in 1872, the losing Democratic candidate for President, Horace Greeley, died shortly after Election Day and before the electors met. Three of his electors insisted on voting for him. Congress would not count these votes for a dead man. Some of the remaining Greeley electors voted for the party's vice-presidential candidate. The rest gave their votes to another Democrat whose name was not on the party's ticket.

THE PRESIDENTIAL SUCCESSION [18]

Representative [now Senator] A. S. Mike Monroney of Oklahoma, one of our ablest congressmen, has recently proposed a constitutional amendment looking to the election of two Vice Presidents instead of one. The suggestion is not novel. In 1881 Representative Hammond of Georgia introduced a resolution providing for the election of three Vice Presidents; in 1886 Representative Dibble of South Carolina would have settled for two. Analagous propositions have been offered in Congress since 1864, when Senator Davis of Kentucky suggested that any vacancy in the office of Vice President should be filled by the Senate from their own number.

All these proposals imply one thing: dissatisfaction with the law governing the presidential succession in the event that both the offices of President and Vice President become vacant. From 1792 to 1886 the officer designated by Congress, under the Constitution, as heir-apparent was the President pro tempore of the Senate; ... [from] 1886 [until 1947] it ... [was] the Secretary of State.

I submit that all of these amendments are wrongly conceived and that if any one of them were to be adopted, the situation would be worse than it is now [before enactment of the Presidential Succession Law of 1947, which does not, however, meet all objections raised in this article]. For they are grounded on the idea that it is better to have a Throttlebottom as President, for what might be the whole of four years, than an Acting President designated by Congress to hold office only "until a President shall be elected"—a constitutional expression which permits, if it does not require, a new election immediately after the death, resignation, or removal of the President.

Take the amendment proposed by Mr. Monroney and assume that both the President and First Vice President die. The Second Vice President would then succeed, and what would this officer be? An exact replica of our present Vice Presidents. Elected

[18] From an article by Lucius Wilmerding, Jr., member of the Institute for Advanced Study, Princeton, N.J. *Atlantic Monthly.* 179:91-7. May 1947. Reprinted by permission.

in the same way to perform the same duties (he is to be President of the Senate, while the First Vice President is to be an executive assistant to the President) he would be, like them, a "secondary character."

I do not mean to suggest that there is no difficulty. I think that there is, and that it is much more immediate and much more serious than that with which Mr. Monroney is dealing. I mean the difficulty of the vice-presidential succession itself. After all, it will seldom happen that both a President and a Vice President will die before the expiration of their four-year term. . . . [It would have happened if Willkie and McNary had been elected in 1940.—Ed.]. . .

This issue is clear: to resolve it we need only to understand what the office of Vice President is and how it is filled. The solution of our difficulty is to be found not in two Vice Presidents but in none.

The office of Vice President has no duties. True the Vice President is President of the Senate and, as such, performs duties analogous to those of the Speaker of the House. But the two offices are separate and distinct. "I am possessed," said John Adams, "of two separate powers; the one in *esse* and the other in *posse*. I am Vice President. In this I am nothing, but I may be everything. But I am President also of the Senate." The combination of offices has excited surprise. Roger Sherman explained it in the Federal Convention: "If the Vice President were not to be President of the Senate, he would be without employment." . . .

Still, if the office is unimportant, the officer is not. As Senator White [of Delaware in 1803] pointed out . . . , "the Vice President is not only the second officer of Government in point of rank but of importance, and should be a man possessing and worthy of the confidence of the nation." Why? Because, to repeat the remark of our first Vice President, he is nothing but he may be everything. And it is particularly to be noted that the Vice President succeeds for the residue of the term, which may be the full four years if the President should die between his election and the date set for his inauguration. . . .

It has been thought extraordinary that the Constitution, as originally adopted, did not provide for a separate vote for the office of Vice President, and prescribed no qualifications for that officer. The explanation is simple. The Vice President was voted for as President and his qualifications were those of the President. . . .

On paper, the plan seemed perfect. In practice, however, it was soon discovered that great inconvenience might arise from this mode of election, and that it might not carry into effect the will of the people as expressed through the electors. The trouble was that the electors did not in fact cast two undistinguishing votes for President, but discriminated in their minds between the persons whom they wanted for President and Vice President, casting one vote for each. . . .

The attempt to choose the Vice President separately from the President destroyed the electoral system. For it made possible, in a particular circumstance, the election of a President and Vice President of opposite political parties. The case occurred in 1796 [John Adams and Jefferson] and was immediately seen to be an evil, at least by the majority party. It might have occurred again in 1804, and to prevent the repetition was the avowed purpose of the Twelfth Amendment. . . .

The Twelfth Amendment, adopted in 1804, provided that each elector was to name in distinct ballots the persons voted for as President and Vice President. When the votes were counted, the person having the greatest number of votes for President was to be President and the person having the greatest number of votes for Vice President was to be Vice President. That—somewhat simplified by the omission of some complicated provisions for throwing the election into the House or the Senate in the event that no candidate obtains a majority vote—is the essence of the Twelfth Amendment. . . .

The Twelfth Amendment has nullified the intention which led to the creation of the vice-presidency. The declared object of the Twelfth Amendment was to prevent a man not intended to be President from being President. Well and good. But when the President dies, the officer whom it was intended to be defeated is promoted; the man whom the people never intended should be

President, who received not one vote for that office, the Vice President, becomes President. Could anything be more ridiculous? . . .

Yet an easy remedy is at hand. Abolish the office—wipe it clean out of the Constitution; provide by law—no further constitutional amendment would be needed—for a new election in the event of the President's death, resignation, or removal; and let Congress declare—as it now declares in providing for the case of a double vacancy—what officer shall act as President until a President be elected or, if the President's disability be merely temporary, until the disability be removed. . . .

The idea of holding an election at other than the fixed periods is not so novel as it may appear. It is contemplated by the Constitution for the case in which both the offices of President and Vice President become vacant. The Vice President succeeds for the remainder of the President's term only because, in the original mode of appointing him, he was expected to be the man in whom the nation reposed its second confidence; in his case a new election could not be necessary. . . .

One difficulty may be specially noticed. It has been objected that an intermediate election might destroy the regular timing of elections at which the President is chosen along with the whole of the House of Representatives and a third of the Senate. The Constitution requires the President to be elected for four years, so that if the timing were once upset it could not easily be restored. . . . If we are about amending the Constitution, any number of remedies could be devised. . . .

But perhaps the simplest expedient of all, the one most in harmony with our existing Constitution, would be to provide that the new election—for a full four-year term—should take place in conjunction with the next Congressional election. The synchronism would be maintained, for the whole of the House and a third of the Senate change every two years, not every four; some senators who expected to ride into office on the coattails of a President might be disappointed, but an equal number would be gratified; and the maximum term of an acting President would be reduced from four years to two—a very sensible advantage.

One question remains to be discussed. Who should be acting President in case of an absolute vacancy in the executive? The question has been much agitated. It was raised in the Federal Convention and much debated before the institution of a vice-presidency reduced its urgency; and it has been much debated since in connection with the secondary succession—the designation by Congress of an officer to act as President when both the offices of President and Vice President are vacant. . . .

Various officers have been suggested as appropriate successors. In the Federal Convention, Hamilton and the Committee of Detail proposed the President of the Senate (this was before the invention of the vice-presidency) ; Gouverneur Morris preferred the Chief Justice; Madison a Cabinet Council if such a body were agreed upon. In the First and Second Congresses the relative merits of the President pro tempore of the Senate, the Speaker of the House, the Chief Justice, the Senior Associate Justice, the Secretary of State, and the Secretary of the Treasury were descanted upon. The ground has frequently been gone over: in 1853 when Vice President King died; in 1868 when the conviction of Johnson would have made Ben Wade President; in 1881 when there was an absolute failure in the succession—no President pro tempore of the Senate and no Speaker of the House —a situation which had occurred in 1877 and 1845; in 1885 when the death of Cleveland would have brought a Republican into the presidency—a situation which had also occurred in Fillmore's time; and in 1945 when Mr. Truman's death would have brought in Mr. Stettinius.

No one can read the elaborate arguments pro and con these various officers without being struck by their weakness. The President pro tempore of the Senate and the Speaker of the House are objected to as not being "officers"; the legislative construction of the Second Congress that they are should be conclusive. The same officers are recommended as being more nearly connected with the people than the Secretary of State. But who is more likely to command the confidence of the people—a man chosen in one state or one district with no thought of the presidency in mind, and who may represent views precisely the opposite of him whom the people as a whole have elected, or a man appointed by the President for the sole purpose of carrying his views into execution? It is also said that no man should appoint his own successor. But why not, provided the successor be only temporary?

It is worthy of remark that these arguments have never had any real weight in determining the succession. The question has always, though improperly, been decided on the basis of personalities.

APPENDIX

THE CONSTITUTION [1]

ARTICLE II.

Section. I. The executive Power shall be vested in a President of the United States of America. He shall hold his Office during the Term of Four Years, and, together with the Vice President, chosen for the same Term, be elected, as follows

Each State shall appoint, in such Manner as the Legislature thereof may direct, a Number of Electors, equal to the whole Number of Senators and Representatives to which the State may be entitled in the Congress: but no Senator or Representative, or Person holding an Office of Trust or Profit under the United States, shall be appointed an Elector. . . .

The Congress may determine the Time of choosing the Electors, and the Day on which they shall give their Votes; which Day shall be the same throughout the United States. . . .

TWELFTH AMENDMENT

The Electors shall meet in their respective states, and vote by ballot for President and Vice President, one of whom, at least, shall not be an inhabitant of the same state with themselves; they shall name in their ballots the person voted for as President, and in distinct ballots the person voted for as Vice President, and they shall make distinct lists of all persons voted for as President, and of all persons voted for as Vice President, and of the number of votes for each, which lists they shall sign and certify, and transmit sealed to the seat of the government of the United States, directed to the President of the Senate;—The President of the Senate shall, in the presence of the Senate and House of Representatives, open all the certificates and the votes shall then be counted;—The person having the greatest number of votes for President, shall be the President, if such number be a majority of the whole number of Electors appointed; and if no person have such majority, then from the persons having the highest numbers not exceeding three on the list of those voted for as President, the House of Representatives shall choose immediately, by ballot, the

[1] From *United States Government Organization Manual 1952-53;* revised as of July 1, 1952. Superintendent of Documents. Washington, D.C. p5-6, 12-13, 15, 16.

President. But in choosing the President, the votes shall be taken by states, the representation from each state having one vote; a quorum for this purpose shall consist of a member or members from two-thirds of the states, and a majority of all the states shall be necessary to a choice. . . . The person having the greatest number of votes as Vice President, shall be the Vice President, if such number be a majority of the whole number of Electors appointed, and if no person have a majority, then from the two highest numbers on the list, the Senate shall choose the Vice President; a quorum for the purpose shall consist of two-thirds of the whole number of Senators, and a majority of the whole number shall be necessary to a choice. But no person constitutionally ineligible to the office of President shall be eligible to that of Vice President of the United States.

FOURTEENTH AMENDMENT

Section 3. No person shall be . . . elector of President and Vice President . . . who, having previously taken an oath, as a member of Congress, or as an officer of the United States, or as a member of any State legislature, or as an executive or judicial officer of any State, to support the Constitution of the United States, shall have engaged in insurrection or rebellion against the same, or given aid or comfort to the enemies thereof. But Congress may by a vote of two-thirds of each House, remove such disability.

TWENTIETH AMENDMENT

Section 1. The terms of the President and Vice President shall end at noon on the 20th day of January, and the terms of Senators and Representatives at noon on the 3d day of January, of the years in which such terms would have ended if this article had not been ratified; and the terms of their successors shall then begin.

Sec. 2. The Congress shall assemble at least once in every year, and such meeting shall begin at noon on the 3d day of January, unless they shall by law appoint a different day.

Sec. 3. If, at the time fixed for the beginning of the term of the President, the President elect shall have died, the Vice President elect shall become President. If a President shall not have been chosen before the time fixed for the beginning of his term, or if the President elect shall have failed to qualify, then the Vice President elect shall act as President until a President shall have qualified; and the Congress may by law provide for the case wherein neither a President elect nor a Vice President elect shall have qualified, declaring who shall then act as President, or the manner in which one who is to act shall be selected, and such person shall act accordingly until a President or Vice President shall have qualified.

Sec. 4. The Congress may by law provide for the case of the death of any of the persons from whom the House of Representatives may choose a President whenever the right of choice shall have devolved upon them, and for the case of the death of any of the persons from whom the Senate may choose a Vice President whenever the right of choice shall have devolved upon them.

TWENTY-SECOND AMENDMENT

No person shall be elected to the office of the President more than twice, and no person who has held the office of President, or acted as President, for more than two years of a term to which some other person was elected President shall be elected to the office of the President more than once. But this Article shall not apply to any person holding the office of President when this Article was proposed by the Congress, and shall not prevent any person who may be holding the office of President, or acting as President, during the term within which this Article becomes operative from holding the office of President or acting as President during the remainder of such term.

PUBLIC LAW 771—80TH CONGRESS [2]

AN ACT

To codify and enact into law Title 3 of the United States Code, entitled "The President".

CHAPTER 1—PRESIDENTIAL ELECTIONS AND VACANCIES

TIME OF APPOINTING ELECTORS

§ 1. The electors of President and Vice President shall be appointed, in each State, on the Tuesday next after the first Monday in November, in every fourth year succeeding every election of a President and Vice President.

FAILURE TO MAKE CHOICE ON PRESCRIBED DAY

§ 2. Whenever any State has held an election for the purpose of choosing electors, and has failed to make a choice on the day prescribed

[2] From *Presidential Election;* provisions of the Constitution and of the United States Code. (Publication 3261) Division of the Public Affairs. Department of State. Superintendent of Documents. Washington, D.C. 1948. p4-12.

by law, the electors may be appointed on a subsequent day in such a manner as the legislature of such State may direct.

NUMBER OF ELECTORS

§ 3. The number of electors shall be equal to the number of Senators and Representatives to which the several States are by law entitled at the time when the President and Vice President to be chosen come into office; except, that where no apportionment of Representatives has been made after any enumeration, at the time of choosing electors, the number of electors shall be according to the then existing apportionment of Senators and Representatives.

VACANCIES IN ELECTORAL COLLEGE

§ 4. Each State may, by law, provide for the filling of any vacancies which may occur in its college of electors when such college meets to give its electoral vote.

DETERMINATION OF CONTROVERSY AS TO APPOINTMENT OF ELECTORS

§ 5. If any State shall have provided, by laws enacted prior to the day fixed for the appointment of the electors, for its final determination of any controversy or contest concerning the appointment of all or any of the electors of such State, by judicial or other methods or procedures, and such determination shall have been made at least six days before the time fixed for the meeting of the electors, such determination made pursuant to such law so existing on said day, and made at least six days prior to said time of meeting of the electors, shall be conclusive, and shall govern in the counting of the electoral votes as provided in the Constitution, and as hereinafter regulated, so far as the ascertainment of the electors appointed by such State is concerned.

CREDENTIALS OF ELECTORS; TRANSMISSION TO SECRETARY OF STATE AND TO CONGRESS; PUBLIC INSPECTION

§ 6. It shall be the duty of the executives of each State, as soon as practicable after the conclusion of the appointment of the electors in such State by the final ascertainment, under and in pursuance of the laws of such State providing for such ascertainment, to communicate by registered mail under the seal of the State to the Secretary of State of the United States a certificate of such ascertainment of the electors appointed, setting forth the names of such electors and the canvass or other ascertainment under the laws of such State of the number of votes given or cast for each person for whose appointment any and all votes have been given or cast; and it shall also thereupon be the duty of the executive of each State to deliver to the electors of such State, on or before the day on which they are required by section 7 of this title to meet, six duplicate-originals of the same certificate under the seal of the State; and if there shall have been any final determination in a State in the manner, provided for by law of a controversy or contest concerning the appointment of all or any of the electors of such State, it shall be the duty of the executive of such State, as soon as practicable after such determination, to communicate under the seal of the State to the Secretary of State of the United States a certificate of such determination in form and manner as the same shall have been made; and the certificate or certificates so received by the Secretary of State shall be preserved by him for one year and shall be a part of the public records of his office and shall be open to public inspection; and the Secretary of State of the United States at the first meeting of Congress thereafter shall transmit to the two Houses of Congress copies in full of each and every such certificate so received at the State Department.

Meeting and Vote of Electors

§ 7. The electors of President and Vice President of each State shall meet and give their votes on the first Monday after the second Wednesday in December next following their appointment at such place in each State as the legislature of such State shall direct.

Manner of Voting

§ 8. The electors shall vote for President and Vice President, respectively, in the manner directed by the Constitution.

Certificates of Votes for President and Vice President

§ 9. The electors shall make and sign six certificates of all the votes given by them, each of which certificates shall contain two distinct lists, one of the votes for President and the other of the vote for Vice President, and shall annex to each of the certificates one of the lists of the electors which shall have been furnished to them by direction of the executive of the State.

Sealing and Endorsing Certificates

§ 10. The electors shall seal up the certificates so made by them, and certify upon each that the lists of all the votes of such State given for President, and of all the votes given for Vice President, are contained therein.

Disposition of Certificates

§ 11. The electors shall dispose of the certificates so made by them and the lists attached thereto in the following manner:

First.   They shall forthwith forward by registered mail one of the same to the President of the Senate at the seat of government.

Second.   Two of the same shall be delivered to the secretary of state of the State, one of which shall be held subject to the order of the President of the Senate, the other to be preserved by him for one year and shall be a part of the public records of his office and shall be open to public inspection.

Third.   On the day thereafter they shall forward by registered mail two of such certificates and lists to the Secretary of State at the seat of government, one of which shall be held subject to the order of the President of the Senate.   The other shall be preserved by the Secretary of State for one year and shall be a part of the public records of his office and shall be open to public inspection.

Fourth.   They shall forthwith cause the other of the certificates and lists to be delivered to the judge of the district in which the electors shall have assembled.

FAILURE OF CERTIFICATES OF ELECTORS TO REACH PRESIDENT OF SENATE OR SECRETARY OF STATE; DEMAND ON STATE FOR CERTIFICATE

§ 12.   When no certificate of vote and list mentioned in sections 9 and 11 of this title from any State shall have been received by the President of the Senate or by the Secretary of State by the fourth Wednesday in December, after the meeting of the electors shall have been held, the President of the Senate or, if he be absent from the seat of government, the Secretary of State shall request, by the most expeditious method available, the secretary of state of the State to send up the certificate and list lodged with him by the electors of such State; and it shall be his duty upon receipt of such request immediately to transmit same by registered mail to the President of the Senate at the seat of government.

SAME; DEMAND ON DISTRICT JUDGE FOR CERTIFICATE

§ 13.   When no certificates of votes from any State shall have been received at the seat of government on the fourth Wednesday in December, after the meeting of the electors shall have been held, the President of the Senate or, if he be absent from the seat of government, the Secretary of State shall send a special messenger to the district judge in whose custody one certificate of votes from that State has been lodged, and such judge shall forthwith transmit that list by the hand of such messenger to the seat of government.

FORFEITURE FOR MESSENGER'S NEGLECT OF DUTY

§ 14.   Every person who, having been appointed, pursuant to section 13 of this title, to deliver the certificates of the votes of the electors to the President of the Senate, and having accepted such appointment, shall neglect to perform the services required from him, shall forfeit the sum of $1,000.

COUNTING ELECTORAL VOTES IN CONGRESS

§ 15. Congress shall be in session on the sixth day of January succeeding every meeting of the electors. The Senate and House of Representatives shall meet in the Hall of the House of Representatives at the hour of 1 o'clock in the afternoon on that day, and the President of the Senate shall be their presiding officer. Two tellers shall be previously appointed on the part of the Senate and two on the part of the House of Representatives, to whom shall be handed, as they are opened by the President of the Senate, all the certificates and papers purporting to be certificates of the electoral votes, which certificates and papers shall be opened, presented, and acted upon in the alphabetical order of the States, beginning with the letter A; and said tellers, having then read the same in the presence and hearing of the two Houses, shall make a list of the votes as they shall appear from the said certificates; and the votes having been ascertained and counted according to the rules in this subchapter provided, the result of the same shall be delivered to the President of the Senate, who shall thereupon announce the state of the vote, which announcement shall be deemed a sufficient declaration of the persons, if any, elected President and Vice President of the United States, and, together with a list of the votes, be entered on the Journals of the two Houses. Upon such reading of any such certificate or paper, the President of the Senate shall call for objections, if any. Every objection shall be made in writing, and shall state clearly and concisely, and without argument, the ground thereof, and shall be signed by at least one Senator and one Member of the House of Representatives before the same shall be received. When all objections so made to any vote or paper from a State shall have been received and read, the Senate shall thereupon withdraw, and such objections shall be submitted to the Senate for its decision; and the Speaker of the House of Representatives shall, in like manner, submit such obections [objections] to the House of Representatives for its decision; and no electoral vote or votes from any State which shall have been regularly given by electors whose appointment has been lawfully certified to according to section 6 of this title from which but one return has been received shall be rejected, but the two Houses concurrently may reject the vote or votes when they agree that such vote or votes have not been so regularly given by electors whose appointment has been so certified. If more than one return or paper purporting to be a return from a State shall have been received by the President of the Senate, those votes, and those only, shall be counted which shall have been regularly given by the electors who are shown by the determination mentioned in section 5 of this title to have been appointed, if the determination in said section provided for shall have been made, or by such successors or substitutes, in case of a vacancy in the board of electors so ascertained, as have been appointed to fill such vacancy in the mode provided by the laws of the State; but in case there shall arise the question which of two or more of such State authorities determining what electors have been appointed, as mentioned in section 5 of this title, is the lawful tribunal of such State, the votes regularly given of those electors, and those only, of such State shall be counted whose title as electors the two Houses, acting separately, shall concurrently decide is supported by the decision of such State so authorized by its law; and in such case of more than one return or paper purporting to be a return from a State, if there shall have been no such determination of the question in the State aforesaid, then those votes, and those only, shall be counted which the two Houses shall concurrently decide were cast by lawful electors appointed in accordance with the laws of the State, unless the two Houses, acting separately, shall concurrently decide such votes not to be the lawful votes of the legally appointed electors of such State. But if the two Houses shall disagree in respect of the counting of such votes, then, and in that case, the votes of the electors whose appointment shall have been certified by the executive of the State, under the seal thereof, shall be counted. When the two Houses have voted, they shall immediately again meet, and the presiding officer shall then announce the decision of the questions submitted. No votes or papers from any other State shall be acted upon until the objections previously made to the votes or papers from any State shall have been finally disposed of.

Same; Seats for Officers and Members of Two Houses in Joint Meeting

§ 16. At such joint meeting of the two Houses seats shall be provided as follows: For the President of the Senate, the Speaker's chair, for the Speaker, immediately upon his left; the Senators, in the body of the Hall upon the right of the presiding officer; for the Representatives, in the body of the Hall not provided for the Senators; for the tellers, Secretary of the Senate, and Clerk of the House of Representatives, at the Clerk's desk; for the other officers of the two Houses, in front of the Clerk's desk and upon each side of the Speaker's platform. Such joint meeting shall not be dissolved until the count of electoral votes shall be completed and the result declared; and no recess shall be taken unless a question shall have arisen in regard to counting any such votes, or otherwise under this subchapter, in which case it shall be competent for either House, acting separately, in the manner hereinbefore provided, to direct a recess of such House not beyond the next calendar day, Sunday excepted, at the hour of 10 o'clock in the forenoon. But if the counting of the electoral votes and the declaration of the result shall not have been completed before the fifth calendar day next after such first meeting of the two Houses, no further or other recess shall be taken by either House.

Same; Limit of Debate in Each House

§ 17. When the two Houses separate to decide upon an objection that may have been made to the counting of any electoral vote or votes from any State, or other question arising in the matter, each Senator and Representative may speak to such objection or question five minutes, and not more than once; but after such debate shall have lasted two hours it shall be the duty of the presiding officer of each House to put the main question without further debate.

Same; Parliamentary Procedure at Joint Meeting

§ 18. While the two Houses shall be in meeting as provided in this subchapter, the President of the Senate shall have power to preserve order; and no debate shall be allowed and no question shall be put by the presiding officer except to either House on a motion to withdraw.

Vacancy in Offices of Both President and Vice President; Officers Eligible to Act

§ 19. (a) (1) If, by reason of death, resignation, removal from office, inability, or failure to qualify, there is neither a President nor Vice President to discharge the powers and duties of the office of President, then the Speaker of the House of Representatives shall, upon his resignation as Speaker and as Representative in Congress, act as President.

(2) The same rule shall apply in the case of the death, resignation, removal from office, or inability of an individual acting as President under this subsection.

(b) If, at the time when under subsection (a) of this section a Speaker is to begin the discharge of the powers and duties of the office of President, there is no Speaker, or the Speaker fails to qualify as Acting President, then the President pro tempore of the Senate shall, upon his resignation as President pro tempore and as Senator, act as president.

(c) An individual acting as President under subsection (a) or subsection (b) of this section shall continue to act until the expiration of the then current Presidential term, except that—

(1) if his discharge of the powers and duties of the office is founded in whole or in part on the failure of both the President-elect and the Vice-President-elect to qualify, then he shall act only until a President or Vice President qualifies; and

(2) if his discharge of the powers and duties of the office is founded in whole or in part on the inability of the President or Vice President, then he shall act only until the removal of the disability of one of such individuals.

(d) (1) If, by reason of death, resignation, removal from office, inability, or failure to qualify, there is no President pro tempore to act as President under subsection (b) of this section, then the officer of the United States who is highest on the following list, and who is not under disability to discharge the powers and duties of the office of President shall act as President: Secretary of State, Secretary of the Treasury, Secretary of Defense, Attorney General, Postmaster General, Secretary of the Interior, Secretary of Agriculture, Secretary of Commerce, Secretary of Labor.

(2) An individual acting as President under this subsection shall continue so to do until the expiration of the then current Presidential term, but not after a qualified and prior-entitled individual is able to act, except that the removal of the disability of an individual higher on the list contained in paragraph (1) of this subsection or the ability to qualify on the part of an individual higher on such list shall not terminate his service.

(3) The taking of the oath of office by an individual specified in the list in paragraph (1) of this subsection shall be held to constitute his resignation from the office by virtue of the holding of which he qualifies to act as President.

(e) Subsections (a), (b), and (d) of this section shall apply only to such officers as are eligible to the office of President under the Constitution. Subsection (d) of this section shall apply only to officers appointed, by and with the advice and consent of the Senate, prior to the time of the death, resignation, removal from office, inability, or failure to qualify, of the President pro tempore, and only to officers not under impeachment by the House of Representatives at the time the powers and duties of the office of President devolve upon them.

(f) During the period that any individual acts as President under this section, his compensation shall be at the rate then provided by law in the case of the President.

RESIGNATION OR REFUSAL OF OFFICE

§ 20. The only evidence of a refusal to accept, or of a resignation of the office of President or Vice President, shall be an instrument in writing, declaring the same, and subscribed by the person refusing to accept or resigning, as the case may be, and delivered into the office of the Secretary of State.

Sec. 2. The provisions of title 3, "The President", set out in section 1 of this Act, shall be construed as a continuation of existing law and no loss of rights, interruption of jurisdiction, nor prejudice to matters pending on the effective date of this Act shall result from its enactment. . . .

LODGE-GOSSETT PLAN [3]

(H. Joint Resolution 2, 81st Congress, 1st Session)

Resolved by the Senate and House of Representatives of the United States of America in Congress assembled (two-thirds of each House concurring therein), That an amendment is hereby proposed to the Constitu-

[3] From *Amend the Constitution with Respect to Election of President and Vice President;* hearings before Subcommittee no 1 of the House Judiciary Committee, February 9, 10, 11, 16 and 25, 1949, on H. Joint Resolutions 2, 10, 11, 51, 74, 78, 81, 82, 118, and 121. 81st Congress, 1st session. Superintendent of Documents. Washington, D.C. 1949. p 1.

tion of the United States which shall be valid to all intents and purposes as part of the Constitution when ratified by three-fourths of the legislatures of the several States. Said amendment shall be as follows:

Section 1. The executive power shall be vested in a President of the United States of America. He shall hold his office during the term of four years, and together with the Vice President, chosen for the same term, be elected as herein provided.

The Electoral College system for electing the President and Vice President of the United States is hereby abolished. The President and Vice President shall be elected by the people of the several States. The electors in each State shall have the qualifications requisite for electors of the most numerous branch of the State legislature. Congress shall determine the time of such election, which shall be the same throughout the United States. Until otherwise determined by the Congress, such election shall be held on the Tuesday next after the first Monday in November of the year preceding the year in which the regular term of the President is to begin. Each State shall be entitled to a number of electoral votes equal to the whole number of Senators and Representatives to which such State may be entitled in the Congress.

Within forty-five days after such election, or at such time as the Congress shall direct, the official custodian of the election returns of each State shall make distinct lists of all persons for whom votes were cast for President and the number of votes for each, and the total vote of the electors of the State for all persons for President, which lists he shall sign and certify and transmit sealed to the seat of the Government of the United States, directed to the President of the Senate. The President of the Senate shall in the presence of the Senate and House of Representatives open all certificates and the votes shall then be counted. Each person for whom votes were cast for President in each State shall be credited with such proportion of the electoral votes thereof as he received of the total vote of the electors therein for President. In making the computations, fractional numbers of less than one one-thousandth shall be disregarded unless a more detailed calculation would change the result of the election. The person having the greatest number of electoral votes for President shall be President. If two or more persons shall have an equal and the highest number of such votes, then the one for whom the greatest number of popular votes were cast shall be President.

The Vice President shall be likewise elected, at the same time and in the same manner and subject to the same provisions, as the President, but no person constitutionally ineligible for the office of President shall be eligible to that of Vice President of the United States.

Sec. 2. Paragraphs 1, 2 and 3 of section 1, article II, of the Constitution and the twelfth article of amendment to the Constitution, are hereby repealed.

Sec. 3. This article shall be inoperative unless it shall have been ratified as an amendment to the Constitution by the legislatures of three-fourths of the States within seven years from the date of the submission hereof to the States by the Congress.

THE COUDERT PROPOSAL [4]

Be it enacted by the Senate and House of Representatives of the United States of America in Congress assembled (two-thirds of each House concurring therein), that the following article is hereby proposed as part of the Constitution of the United States, which shall be valid to all intents and purposes as part of the Constitution when ratified by the legislatures of three-fourths of the several States:

Section 1. Each State shall choose a number of electors of the President and Vice President, equal to the whole number of Senators and Representatives to which the State may be entitled in the Congress, in the same manner as its Senators and Representatives are chosen. But no Senator or Representative or person holding an office of trust or profit under the United States shall be chosen elector.

Sec. 2. The electors shall meet in their respective States, and vote by ballot for President and Vice President, one of whom, at least, shall not be an inhabitant of the same State with themselves; they shall name in their ballots the persons voted for as President, and in distinct ballots the person voted for as Vice President; and they shall make distinct list of all persons voted for as President, and of all persons voted for as Vice President, and of the number of votes for each, which list they shall sign and certify, and transmit sealed to the seat of government of the United States, directed to the President of the Senate; the President of the Senate shall, in the presence of the Senate and the House of Representatives, open all the certificates and the votes shall then be counted; the person having the greatest number of votes for President shall be the President and the person having the greatest number of votes for Vice President shall be the Vice President, if such numbers be majorities of the whole number of electors chosen.

Sec. 3. If no persons voted for as President or Vice President have a majority of the whole number of electors chosen, then from the persons having the highest numbers, not exceeding three, on the lists of those voted for as President and Vice President, the Senate and the House of Representatives, assembled and voting as one body, shall choose immediately the President, and then the Vice President, or either, as the case may be; a quorum for these purposes shall consist of three-fourths of the whole number of the Senators and Representatives, and the persons receiving the greatest number of votes for President and for Vice Presi-

[4] From H. Joint Resolution 1, introduced by Representative Frederic Coudert (Republican, New York) January 3, 1953, which was referred to the House Judiciary Committee. 83d Congress, 1st session. Superintendent of Documents. Washington, D.C. 1953. p 1-3. Reprinted from a copy provided by Representative Coudert.

dent on the respective roll calls shall be the President and the Vice President. But no person ineligible to the office of President shall be eligible to the office of Vice President.

SENATOR SMATHERS' PROPOSAL [5]

Section 1. Effective one year after the ratification of this article for all presidential elections occurring thereafter, political parties' nominees for President and Vice President shall be nominated in simultaneous, nation-wide individual party primaries for which Congress shall have the power to enact appropriate legislation.

Sec. 2. For the purposes of this article a political party shall be recognized as such if at any time within four years next preceding a primary election it has had registered as members thereof more than 10 per cent of the total registered voters in the United States.

Sec. 3. Voters in each State shall have the qualifications requisite for voters of the most numerous branch of the State legislature but each voter shall be eligible to vote only in the primary of the party of his registered affiliation.

Sec. 4. No person shall be a candidate for nomination except in the primary of the party of his registered affiliation and his name shall be on that party's ballot in all the States.

Sec. 5. The determination of the nominees for President and Vice President of each party shall be computed on the same basis as the then existing method of electing the President and Vice President of the United States, except that in the absence of a majority for any one candidate a second primary shall determine the nominee.

Sec. 6. This article shall be inoperative unless it shall have been ratified as an amendment to the Constitution by the legislatures of three-fourths of the several States within seven years from the date of its submission.

[5] S. Joint Resolution 8, 83d Congress, 1st session. *Congressional Record.* 99: (daily) 162. January 7, 1953.

BIBLIOGRAPHY

An asterisk (*) preceding a reference indicates that the article or a part of it has been reprinted in this book.

BOOKS AND PAMPHLETS

Albright, Spencer D. American ballot. 153p. Public Affairs Press. Washington 8, D.C. '42.

Aly, Bower, ed. Presidential elections. (National University Extension Association. Committee on debate materials and interstate cooperation. Debate handbook 23. 1949-1950) 2v. 220p. each. Lucas Brothers. Columbia, Mo. '49.

Aly, Bower, ed. Selecting the President. (National University Extension Association. Committee on debate materials and interstate cooperation. Debate handbook 27. 1953-1954) 2v. 220p. each. Lucas Brothers. Columbia, Mo. '53.

American Institute of Public Opinion, comp. Gallup political almanac for 1946. The Institute. Princeton, N.J. '46.

Arnold, J. H. Debater's guide. Handy Book Corporation. Harrisburg, Pa. '23.
> See "Resolved, that the president should be elected by direct vote of the people." p302-3. Brief pros and cons, and references.

Beard, C. A. American government and politics. 9th ed. 872p. Macmillan Co. New York. '41.

Beard, William. Government and liberty; the American system. 362p. Halcyon House. Garden City, N.Y. '47.

Beman, L. T. comp. Abolishment of the electoral college. (Reference Shelf. v3, no7) 121p. H. W. Wilson Co. New York. '26.

Bernard, B. M. Election laws of the forty-eight states. 96p. (Legal Almanac Series no24) Oceana Publications. 461 W. 18th St. New York. '50.

Bishop, H. M. and Hendel, Samuel. Basic issues of American democracy. 323p. Appleton-Century-Crofts Co. New York. '48.
> See "The presidency," p211-27.

Brogan, D. W. Government of the people; a study of the American political system. Harper & Bros. New York. '43.

Brogan, D. W. Study of politics. 226p. Macmillan Co. New York. '46.

Bryce, James. American commonwealth. abridged ed. 555p. Macmillan Co. New York. '24.

Chamber of Commerce of the State of New York. Presidential succession. 3p. The Chamber. 65 Liberty Street. New York. '47.

Corwin, E. S. Constitution and what it means today. 10th ed. rev. 273p. Princeton University Press. Princeton, N.J. '48.

Corwin, E. S. and Peltason, J. W. Understanding the Constitution. 147p. William Sloane Associates. New York. '49.

Dimock, M. E. and Dimock, G. O. American government in action. 946p. Rinehart & Co. New York. '46.

Fellman, David, ed. Readings in American national government. 300p. Rinehart & Co. New York. '47.

Ferguson, J. H. and McHenry, D. E. American system of government. 972p. McGraw-Hill Book Co. New York. '47.

Gosnell, Harold F. Democracy, the threshold of freedom. 316p. Ronald Press Co. New York. '48.

Herring, Pendleton. Politics of democracy; American parties in action. 468p. Rinehart & Co. New York. '40.

Johnsen, J. E. Direct election of the president. (Reference Shelf. v21, no4) 300p. H. W. Wilson Co. New York. '49.

Johnson, C. O. American national government. 2d ed. 690p. Thomas Y. Crowell Co. New York. '47.

Lea, C. F. Modernize our presidential election. 17p. The Author. 777-14th St., N.W. Washington, 5, D.C. '47.

Levin, P. R. Seven by chance; the accidental presidents. 374p. Farrar, Straus & Co. New York. '48.

Lodge, H. C. ed. Federalist; a commentary on the Constitution of the United States; a collection of essays, reprinted from the original text of Alexander Hamilton, John Jay, and James Madison. G. P. Putnam's Sons. New York. '23.
    See Hamilton, Alexander. "Mode of appointment of the chief magistrate." p423-8.

Lubell, Samuel. Future of American politics. 285p. Harper & Bros. New York. '52.

Maxey, C. C. American problem of government. 5th ed. 651p. Appleton-Century-Crofts. New York. '49.

Meredith, M. R. Practical politics and democracy. 147p. Meador Publishing Co. Boston. '45.

Merriam, C. E. and Gosnell, H. F. American party system; an introduction to the study of political parties in the United States. 4th ed. 530p. Macmillan Co. New York. '49.

Munro, W. B. Government of the United States; national, state and local. 5th ed. 887p. Macmillan Co. New York. '46.

Myers, W. S. Politics and the electoral college. 8p. Committee of Americans. 122 E. 42d St. New York 17. '44.

National Institute of Social Relations. People's choice. (Series G-132). 14p. The Institute. 1244 20th St. Washington 6, D.C. '48.

Odegard, P. H. and Helms, E. A. American politics; a study in political dynamics. 2d ed. 806p. Harper & Bros. New York. '47.

Ogg, F. A. and Ray, P. O. Introduction to American government. 9th ed. rev. 1135p. Appleton-Century-Crofts. New York. '48.

Rousse, T. A. Political ethics and the voter. (Reference Shelf v24, no 1). 181p. H. W. Wilson Co. New York. '52.

Sait, E. M. American parties and elections. 4th ed. by H. R. Penniman. (Century Political Science Series) 668p. D. Appleton-Century Co. New York. '48.

Schattschneider, E. E. Struggle for party government. 46p. University of Maryland, Department of Government and Politics. College Park, Md. '48.

Schlesinger, A. M. Paths to the present. 317p. Macmillan Co. New York. '49.

Shoup, E. L. National government of the American people. 914p. Ginn & Co. Boston. '48.
 See "The electoral system of the United States," p285-313.

Smith, E. C. Dictionary of American politics. 186p. Barnes & Noble. New York. '44.

Stoddard, H. L. Presidential sweepstakes; the story of political conventions and campaigns; ed. by F. W. Leary. 224p. G. P. Putnam's Sons. New York. '48.

Stow, T. J. Presidential election problems. 105p. Dale Publishing Co. Harrison, Ark. '49.

*United States. Department of State. Office of Public Affairs. Presidential elections; provisions of the Constitution and of the United States Code. (Publication 3261) 12p. Supt. of Docs. Washington, D.C. '48.

*United States. House of Representatives. H. Joint Res. 1 introduced by Representative Frederic Coudert, January 3, 1953, which was referred to the House Judiciary Committee. 3p. Supt. of Docs. Washington, D.C. '53.

*United States. House of Representatives. Judiciary Committee. Amend the Constitution to abolish the electoral college system; hearings before a subcommittee on H. Joint Resolution 11, 14, 19, 89, 90, 109, and 205, Apr. 18 and 20, 1951. 337p. 82d Congress, 1st session. Supt. of Docs. Washington, D.C. '51.
 Statements by J. Harvie Williams and Clarence F. Lea, and study by Lucius Wilmerding, Jr. are reprinted in this book.

*United States. House of Representatives. Judiciary Committee. Amend the Constitution with respect to election of President and Vice President; hearings before a subcommittee on H. Joint Resolutions 2, 10, 11, 51, 74, 78, 81, 82, 118, and 121, Feb. 9, 10, 11, 16 and 25, 1949. 289p. 81st Congress, 1st session. Supt. of Docs. Wash. D.C. '49.
 Text of Lodge-Gossett Plan is reprinted in this book.

United States. House of Representatives. Judiciary Committee. Proposing an amendment to the Constitution of the United States providing for the election of President and Vice President; report to accompany H. Joint Resolution 9. (H. Rep. no 1615) 8p. 80th Congress, 2d session. Supt. of Docs. Washington, D.C. Mr. 26, '48.

United States. House of Representatives. Select Committee on Lobbying
Activities. Report and recommendations on Federal lobbying activities. (H. Rep. no3239) 2pts. 58p. and 12p. 81st Congress, 2d
session. Supt. of Docs. Washington, D.C. '51.

United States. House of Representatives. Special Committee to In-
vestigate Campaign Expenditures. Report. 47p. (H. Rep. no3252)
81st Congress. 2d session. Supt. of Docs. Washington, D.C. '51.

*United States. National Archives and Records Service. Federal Regis-
ter Division. United States Government organization manual 1952-
53; revised as of July 1, 1952. 742p. Supt. of Docs. Washington, D.C.

United States. Senate. Electoral college; constitutional provisions and
laws on election of president and vice president, together with the
nomination and election of presidential electors; compiled under the
direction of E. A. Halsey. 26p. (Senate Doc. no243) 78th Congress, 2d session. Supt. of Docs. Washington, D.C. 44.

United States. Senate. Survey of the electoral college in the political
system of the United States. Joseph Jackson. (Senate Doc. no97)
17p. 79th Congress, 1st session. Supt. of Docs. Washington, D.C.
'45.

United States. Senate. Committee on Rules and Administration. Preference primaries for nomination of candidates for President and Vice
President; hearings, before subcommittee on rules, March 28, 1952,
on S. 2570. 153p. 82d Congress, 2d session. Supt. of Docs. Washington, D.C. '52.

United States. Senate. Judiciary Committee. Amending the Constitution with respect to the election of the president and vice president;
hearings, April 26, 1948, on S. Joint Resolution 200. 55p. 80th
Congress, 2d session. Supt. of Docs. Washington, D.C. '48.

*United States. Senate. Judiciary Committee. Election of President
and Vice President; hearings before a subcommittee on S. Joint
Resolution 2, Feb. 23-May 3, 1949. 215p. 81st Congress, 1st
session. The committee. Washington, D.C. '49.
　　Statements by Homer Ferguson and Basil Brewer are reprinted in this
book.

United States. Senate. Judiciary Committee. Proposing amendments to
the Constitution of the United States providing for the election of
president and vice president; report to accompany S. Joint Resolution 200. (S. Rep. no 1230) 5p. 80th Congress, 2d session.
Supt. of Docs. Washington, D.C. '48.

United States. Supreme Court. Official reports of Supreme Court. v335
U.S. 887. Adcock et al. v. Albritton et al. Supt. of Docs. Washington, D.C. '48.

United States. Supreme Court. Official reports of Supreme Court.
v335 U.S. 882. Folsom et al. v. Albritton et al. Supt. of Docs.
Washington, D.C. '48.

Van Doren, Carl. Great rehearsal. 336p. Viking Press. New York. '48.

Wilson, F. G. American political mind. McGraw-Hill Book Co. 506p. New York. '49.
See "The Second Era of Democratic Reform" p327-36.

Wilson, Woodrow. Constitutional government in the United States. 236p. Columbia University; Press. New York. '08.
See "President of the United States." p54-81.

PERIODICALS

Alabama Law Review. 1:40-6. Fall '48. Discretion of president electors. Y. Wilburn.

American Mercury. 75:6-7. Ag. '52. National conventions. H. L. Mencken.

American Mercury. 75:104-7. Ag. '52. People at the polls. Samuel Lubell and James Burnham.

*American Mercury. 75:20-31. O. '52. What price presidents? Serge Fliegers.

American Political Science Review. 41:931-41. O. '47. New presidential succession act. J. E. Kallenbach.

American Political Science Review. 44:86-99. Mr. '50. Lodge-Gossett resolution: a critical analysis. R. C. Silva.

American Political Science Review. 49:872-5. D. '50. Political activity of American Citizens. J. L. Woodward and Elmo Roper.

Annals of the American Academy of Political and Social Science. 259:1-152. S. '48. Parties and politics: 1948. C. C. Rohlfing and J. C. Charlesworth, eds.

*Annals of the American Academy of Political and Social Science. 283:122-6. S. '52. Present party organization and finance. D. E. McHenry.

*Annals of the American Academy of Political and Social Science. 283:127-40. S. '52. Campaign methods today. H. A. Bone.

*Annals of the American Academy of Political and Social Science. 283:156-60. S. '52. Participation in the forthcoming election. H. F. Gosnell.

*Atlantic Monthly. 179:34-40. My. '47. Bosses and machines. E. J. Flynn.

*Atlantic Monthly. 179:91-7. My. '47. Presidential succession. Lucius Wilmerding, Jr.

*Business Week. p24-6. Ja. 26, '52. Convention delegates: how tight are they tied?

Catholic World. 175:406-12. S. '52. Conventions, fact and myth. A. R. Pinci.

Christian Century. 69:301. Mr. 12, '52. Why not nomination by direct primary?

*Christian Century. 69:774. Jl. 2, '52. Optical illusion of politics.

*Collier's. 131:34-9. Ja. 31, '53. Why not let the people elect our president? Estes Kefauver, with S. M. Shalett.

Congressional Digest. 23:178-9, 188-91. Je.-Jl. '44. U.S. electoral college, historic stormy petrel; and pro and con the question of abolishing the electoral college.

Congressional Digest. 27:101-28. Ap. '48. Revived controversy over the electoral college system; fact material and pro and con discussion.

Congressional Digest. 28:193-224. Ag. '49. Should Congress adopt the pending plan for direct election of the president? fact material pro and con discussion.

Congressional Digest. 31:67-96. Mr. '52. U.S. Election process— how it works and what it needs.

Congressional Record. 86:13619-21. N. 15, '40. Constitutional provisions and laws governing election of president and vice president.

Congressional Record. 87:438-41. Ja. 31, '41. Popular election of president and vice president. H. C. Lodge, Jr.

Congressional Record. 87:A5601-2. D. 15, '41. Rocky road to the White House. C. F. Lea.

Congressional Record. 90:3051-3. Je. 5, '44. Abolish the electoral college. Emanuel Celler.

Congressional Record. 90:A3036-7. Je. 15, '44. Bill to amend the Constitution to abolish the electoral college. Emanuel Celler.

Congressional Record. 90:A3088. Je. 17, '44. Electoral college plot.

Congressional Record. 90:6032-6. Je. 23, '44. Electoral college; Senate debate.

Congressional Record. 90:6629-30. Je. 23, '44. Proposed abolition of electoral college method of election of President and vice president. J. F. Guffey.

Congressional Record. 90:A4382-3. N. 14, '44. We should modernize our method of electing the president. C. F. Lea.

Congressional Record. 91:A1104-6. Mr 1, '45. Dangers of our outmoded electoral system. Estes Kefauver.

Congressional Record. 91:A1572-3. Mr. 28, '45. Our accidental presidents. F. T. Wilson.

Congressional Record. 93:(daily)2050-1. Mr. 12, '47. Proposed amendment to the Constitution; text, and statement. W. N. Langer.

Congressional Record. 93:(daily)738-41. Ja. 30, '47. Presidential succession law. Estes Kefauver.

Congressional Record. 93:(daily)A3904-7. Jl. 21, '47. Electors and electoral college. Ed. Gossett.

Congressional Record. 93:(daily)A4230-1. Jl. 28, '47. Voters' revolution. Roscoe Drummond.

Congressional Record. 94:(daily)A1118-20. F. 24, '48. Change our presidential election system so as to make it responsive to the voters and the political parties. Estes Kefauver.

    Same with title Our presidential election system. Vital Speeches of the Day. 14:478-80. My. 15, '48.

Congressional Record. 94:(daily)A1652-3. Mr. 15, '48. Election reform. Fritz Morstein-Marx.

Congressional Record. 94:(daily)3035-6. Mr. 16, '48. Presidential electoral system changed. Estes Kefauver.

Congressional Record. 94:(daily)A2111-13. Mr. 31, '48. Our electoral system is in urgent need of remodeling. Estes Kefauver.
Reprint from Progressive Magazine, April 1948.

Congressional Record. 94:(daily)A2950-2. My. 6, '48. Both Judiciary committees of Congress sponsor the modernization of our presidential elections. C. F. Lea.

Congressional Record. 94:(daily)5601-2. My. 10, '48. No electoral college.

Congressional Record. 94:(daily)5801-2. My. 12, '48. Streamlining the electoral college.

Congressional Record. 94:(daily)6402-3. My. 21, '48. Changing our election system. C. M. Roberts.

Congressional Record. 94:(daily)6614. My. 26, '48. National affairs. T. L. Stokes.

Congressional Record. 94:(daily)A3504-6. My. 27, '48. Counting of electoral votes. H. C. Lodge, Jr.

Congressional Record. 94:(daily)A3568-70. My. 28, '48. Count the votes fairly. C. F. Lea.

Congressional Record. 94:(daily)A3775-6. Je. 7, '48. Appeal to the House leadership to afford members an opportunity to vote on the pending resolution to submit to the states a constitutional amendment to modernize our presidential election. C. F. Lea.

Congressional Record. 94:(daily)A4939-40. Jl. 29, '48. Count of electoral votes; including table of popular votes by states, 1944, together with electoral votes under present system and under S. J. Res. 200. H. C. Lodge, Jr.

Congressional Record. 95:(daily)49. Ja. 5, '49. Change in method of electing president and vice president; statement on S. J. Res. 2. H. C. Lodge, Jr.

Congressional Record. 95:(daily)A197-8. Ja. 17, '49. Counting of electoral votes. H. C. Lodge, Jr.

Congressional Record. 95:(daily)A262-5. Ja. 24, '49. Count of electoral votes; text of S. J. Res. 2, together with letter from Brookings Institution and newspaper comment.

Congressional Record. 95:(daily)A359-61, Ja. 27; A429-31, Ja. 31, '49. Count of electoral votes; newspaper editorials and articles.

Congressional Record. 95:(daily)A1011-12. F. 21, '49. Proposed change in election of a president should have adequate safeguards against minority rule. Wright Patman.

Congressional Record. 95:(daily)A1358-64. Mr. 9, '49. Counting of electoral votes; statements before Senate Committee on the Judiciary. March 9, 1949. Homer Ferguson, Basil Brewer.

Congressional Record. 95:(daily)2946-51. Mr. 22, '49. Proposed abolition of electoral college; questions by Senator Ferguson and answers by Senator Lodge.

Congressional Record. 95:(daily)A1768-70. Mr. 24, '49. Change of method of counting electoral vote for president and vice president. H. C. Lodge, Jr.

Congressional Record. 95:(daily)A1977-8. Mr. 31, '49. Statement before House Committee on the Judiciary, March 31, 1949. J. A. Tawney.

Congressional Record. 95:(daily)3918. Ap. 5, '49. Splinter bogy; editorial from Washington Post.

Congressional Record. 98:578-9. Ja. 29, '52. Remarks by Senator George A. Smathers on the presidential primary system.
        Same condensed. Congressional Digest. 31:84-7. Mr. '52.

*Congressional Record. 99:(daily)161-2. Ja. 7, '53. Remarks by Senator George Smathers.

Current History. 22:75-9. F. '52. Two-party system in the crucible? E. D. Ellis.

Current History. 23:193-245. O. '52. Presidential elections: 1792-1948; symposium.

*Editorial Research Reports. 1, no3:49-59. Ja. 16, '52. Presidential primaries. Roma K. McNickle.

Editorial Research Reports. 1, no2:21-33. Ja. 14, '48. Presidential primaries. B. W. Patch.

*Fortune. 39:138-46. Je. '49. Lodge-Gossett plan. Herbert Wechsler.

'47; the Magazine of the Year. 1:21-4. Ag. '47. Voters' revolution. Roscoe Drummond.

Forum. 112:18-22. Jl. '49. Reform the electoral college! L. F. Allen.

*Forum. 112:224-31. O. '49. Forum: should the president be elected by direct popular vote? J. B. Andrews; T. J. Brown.

Hearst's International Cosmopolitan. 116:54-5+. F. '44. Defeat of democracy. J. N. Baker.
        Condensed, with title How we ought to elect presidents. Reader's Digest. 44:103-4. Mr. '44.

Human Events, 10, no21. D. 10, '52. Electoral reform—the Coudert Amendment. J. Harvie Williams.
        Same. Congressional Record. 99:A65-6. Ja. 9, '53.

Iron Age. 162:127. S. 9, '48. Voters favor changing president electoral system; Gallup poll.

*Journal of the National Education Association. 41:424-5. O. '52. How we elect a President.

Nation. 170:244-45. Mr. 18, '50. Liberals and electoral reform; Lodge-Gossett amendment.

National Municipal Review. 37:344-5. Je. '48. P.R. for presidential electoral votes advances.

National Municipal Review. 39:396-9. S. '50. One way to get out the
    vote. H. J. Abraham.

Nation's Business. 40:104. O. '52. This is our pattern.

Nation's Business. 36:38+. Je. '48. Where pandemonium and politics
    meet. J. B. Wood.

New Republic. 111:596-7. N. 6, '44. We might not have a president.
    Estes Kefauver.

New Republic. 119:7-8. N. 8, '48. If every vote really counted. Car-
    roll Kilpatrick.

New Republic. 122:5-7. F. 27, '50. Electoral college reform.

New York Times. p20. F. 27, '48. Electoral votes are subject to state
    powers; proposal of Governor Tuck to Virginia legislature. Arthur
    Krock.

New York Times. p E8. N. 14, '48. Our electoral college; its aboli-
    tion urged to prevent reversal of popular will. R. H. Wels.

New York Times. p E3. N. 21, '48. Lodge electoral plan protects
    small states. Arthur Krock.

New York Times. p E3. N. 28, '48. Stronger case is made for elec-
    toral reform. Arthur Krock.

New York Times. p26. Ja. 12, '49. Merits of the electoral system;
    inequality between North and South must be accepted. Gelston
    Hinds.

New York Times. p22. Ja. 18, '49. Is the combined 12-20 amend-
    ment a must? Arthur Krock.

*New York Times. p 18. Ap. 25, '52. Supreme Court and the elec-
    toral college. Arthur Krock.

New York Times. p. 14. D. 26, '52. Psychological advantages of
    electoral college. Arthur Krock.
        Same. Congressional Record. 99:A15. Ja. 6, '53. Extension of
    remarks by F. H. Coudert, Jr.

New York Times Magazine. p9+. Mr. 26, '44. It's an obstacle race
    to the White House. J. A. Hagerty.

New York Times Magazine. p 13+. Ap. 27, '47. Only two terms
    for a President? H. S. Commager.

New York Times Magazine. p7+. Jl. 11, '48. Convention system: a
    5-count indictment. James Reston.

New York Times Magazine. p22. Ja. 18, '49. Electoral votes. H. C.
    Lodge, Jr.

New York Times Magazine. p9+. Mr. 16, '52. Indictment of the
    political convention. Estes Kefauver.

*New York Times Magazine. p9+. Ap. 20, '52. Getting nominated
    is an intricate business. T. L. Stokes.

*New York Times Magazine. p9+. Je. 15, '52. Case for the smoke-
    filled room. J. M. Burns.

New York Times Magazine. p 13. S. 7, '52. Our two-party system.
    J. M. Burns.

*New York Times Magazine. p8+. N. 9, '52. Our campaign tech-
    niques reexamined. James Reston.

Newsweek. 16:13-14. D. 23, '40. 531 forgotten men; vote on presidential electors again raises issue of reform.

Newsweek. 33:22. Je. 27, '49. Electoral college dent.

Ohio State Bar Association Report. 17:518-22. Ja. 8, '45. Dangers of our outmoded electoral system and what should be done. Estes Kefauver.

Pathfinder. 60:13. Ja. 7, '53. Mending the political roof. Felix Morley.

 Same. Congressional Record. 99:A35-6. Ja. 7, '53. Extension of remarks by F. H. Coudert.

*Reader's Digest. 60:14-18. F. '52. This year help nominate your presidential candidate. William Hard.

Reviewing Stand (Northwestern University on the Air). 11, no 15:1-11. How important is the electoral college? Mrs. P. H. Douglas, C. S. Hyneman and Roland Young.

*Rotarian. 75:24-5+. Jl. '49. Should the United States abolish the electoral college? H. C. Lodge, Jr.; Wright Patman.

Saturday Evening Post. 213:26. D. 28, '40. Sacred awkwardness.

 Same. Congressional Digest. 20:95-6. Mr. '41.

*Saturday Evening Post. 221:23+. Jl. 10, '48. Do campaigns really change votes? George Gallup and W. A. Lydgate.

Saturday Evening Post. 224:10+. Ja. 12, '52. Americans lead world in avoiding elections.

*Saturday Review of Literature. 34:7-9+. Ap. 7, '51. Crime, reform and the voter. Elmo Roper and Louis Harris.

Science Digest. 16:53-7. N. '44. Electoral college plays tricks with your ballot. M. P. Akers.

 Condensed from Chicago Sun. Ag. 28, 29, 30, '44.

Scientific American. 179:7-11. D. '48. Public opinion polls. Frederick Mosteller and others.

Senior Scholastic. 45:8. O. 23, '44. Electoral college. H. S. Commager.

Senior Scholastic. 53:15. S. 22, '48. Choosing a candidate. H. S. Commager.

*Senior Scholastic. 53:15-16. O. 6, '48. The campaign—our political safety valve. H. S. Commager.

Senior Scholastic. 53:6-7. O. 6, '48. Should we scrap the electoral college?

*Senior Scholastic. 53:17. O. 13, '48. When parties stand or fall. H. S. Commager.

Senior Scholastic. 55:11-12. O. 19, '49. Should we elect the President by popular vote? debate.

Senior Scholastic. 56:12. F. 15, '50. Making votes count.

Senior Scholastic. 61, pt2:13. O. 1, '52. Constitution and the election.

Senior Scholastic. 61, pt2:16-17. O. 1, '52. How the candidates were nominated. David Botter.

Social Studies. 39:291-302. N. '48. Election to the presidency. George Ehnebom.

South Atlantic Quarterly. 47:330-41. Jl. '48. Shall the people elect the president? proposed limitation to two terms. W. S. Jenkins and C. S. James, Jr.

Southwestern Social Science Quarterly. 29:293-8. Mr. '49. Primaries as real elections. C. A. M. Ewing.

State Government. 21:140-3+. Jl. '48. New primary system. J. P. Harris.

Time. 59:25. F. 25, '52 How delegates are chosen.

Time. 59:23. Ap. 28, '52. There ought to be a law.

Town Meeting (Bulletin of America's Town Meeting of the Air). 13, no 15:1-24. Is the two-party system failing in America? George Outland and others. '47.

United States News & World Report. 25:30-1. Jl. 9, '48. Should Presidents control their own renomination? Woodrow Wilson. Letter dated February 5, 1913.

United States News & World Report. 30:58. Ap. 20, '51. We've been asked: How to remove a President.

United States News and World Report. 32:76. Ja. 18, '52. **Let the people nominate.** David Lawrence.

*United States News and World Report. 32:19-21. F. 1, '52. How a President is chosen.

*United States News & World Report. 32:66. F. 22, '52. We've been asked: When Presidents must quit.

*United States News & World Report. 32:40-6. Je. 27, '52. How conventions are run: interview with J. A. Farley.

United States News & World Report. 33:66. O. 31, '52. We've been asked: How the electoral vote works.

*United States News & World Report. 33:84. N. 14, '52. We've been asked: If a president-elect dies—.

Virginia Quarterly Review. 26, no2:268-76. [Ap.] '50. Political competition will help the South. Estes Kefauver.

Vital Speeches of the Day. 13:605-7. Jl. 15, '47. Presidential two-term amendment. D. F. Fleming.

*Vital Speeches of the Day. 18:722-5. S. 14, '52. Let us choose our president on a more equitable basis in 1956. J. I. Dolliver.

World Today. 8:278-87. Jl. '52. United States presidential election; procedure and prospects; the primaries and conventions; the presidential election.

*Yale Review. 34, no3:395-404. [Mr.] '45. Will of the people. Carl Becker.
  Condensed. Congressional Digest. 31:85+. Mr. '52.

Yale Review. 37, no4:619-37. [Je.] '48. American president. C. L. Rossiter.

*Yale Review. 42, no3:410-27. [Mr.] '52. More responsible party system? W. G. Carleton.

SPEECH AND DEBATING

Competitive Debate: Rules and Strategy. By G. M. Musgrave. 151p. rev. ed. 1946. $1.25.

Democracy Through Discussion. By Bruno Lasker. 376p. 1949. $3.50.

Discussion Methods: Explained and Illustrated. By J. V. Garland. 376p. 3d ed. rev. 1951. $3.

Extempore Speaking: A Handbook for the Student, the Coach, and the Judge. By D. L. Holley. 115p. 1947. $1.50.

High School Forensics: An Integrated Program. By A. E. Melzer. 153p. 1946. 90c.

How to Debate. By H. B. Summers, F. L. Whan, and T. A. Rousse. rev. ed. 349p. 1950. $2.75.

Representative American Speeches. By A. C. Baird, comp. Published annually in The Reference Shelf. Prices vary.

Each volume contains representative speeches by eminent men and women on public occasions during the year. Each speech is prefaced by a short sketch of the speaker and the occasion.

Selected Readings in Rhetoric and Public Speaking. By Lester Thonssen, comp. 324p. 1942. $3.50.